Practice Teaching in Social Work

A Handbook

by

Neil Thompson, Martina Osada & Bob Anderson

First Edition – 1990

Second (Revised) Edition – 1994

ISBN 0 948680 36 9

Acknowledgements

In producing the first edition of this text, we had the support and assistance of a number of people and we remain indebted to them for that assistance. Since then, we have had considerable further help, in the form of positive and constructive feedback on the first edition, from a range of people too numerous to mention. In addition, we would like to thank Ruth Tagg, Joyce Thompson, Angela Thompson and Karen Randles for typing the manuscripts.

The Authors

Neil Thompson has extensive experience of practice teaching and now works as a Senior Lecturer in Social Work at the North East Wales Institute of Higher Education. He has previously worked as a social worker, team leader and training officer.

Martina Osada is an Assistant Chief Probation Officer with Northumbria Probation Service. Her interest in practice teaching was also reflected in her previous posts – student unit manager, DipSW development officer at Durham University and a joint appointment with Staffordshire Probation Service and Keele University.

Bob Anderson taught social work at Keele University from 1970 to 1989 and was for several years responsible for running the two-year CQSW course. He now works for Age Concern as its Contracts Unit Co-ordinator.

Contents Guide

Preface   4

Introduction   6

Chapter 1   Patterns of Adult Learning   9

Chapter 2   Teaching Anti-Discriminatory Practice   15

Chapter 3   Pre-placement Planning   25

Chapter 4   Selection of Workload   35

Chapter 5   The Supervisory Process   42

Chapter 6   Methods of Evaluation   50

Chapter 7   Evaluation of Student Performance   59

Chapter 8   Troubleshooting: Dealing with Difficulties   68

Chapter 9   Conclusion   84

Appendices

    1   Placement Request Form   89
    2   Contract Proforma   94
    3   Evaluation Report   98
    4   Positive and Negative Indicators   100

Bibliography   109

Index   111

Preface

All social workers remember their placement experiences during training. For many students struggling to make sense of the theoretical perspectives of the course, the practical placement embodies the rationale for their career choice. It is an opportunity to experience a variety of social work methods, within a range of social work settings, and often with client groups previously unknown. Many students use the placements to extend their knowledge of different client groups and allied agencies; others further their understanding by developing specialist skills in familiar territory.

In general, the practice placement enables students to take supervised and supported risks in extending their own learning and it will often set the pattern for future working methods and professional practice. Clients can benefit through carefully considered and well-delivered practice. Courses can be enriched by the integration of theory and practice and the invaluable feedback that placements provide for future learning needs. Teams and agencies can develop when the student's perspective as a learner questions existing practices and offers a renewed theoretical perspective.

None of this is possible without a good practice teacher.

The role of practice teacher is complex and vital. It incorporates the skills of enabling, supporting, challenging, teaching, managing and evaluating. It requires energy, enthusiasm and commitment, self-awareness and creativity. The practice teacher has to examine and evaluate theoretical perspectives, agency policy, statutory tasks and the political context. This range of tasks cannot be undertaken without the support of colleagues and of the agency. The former can provide encouragement and practical help, share the work and contribute feedback regarding student performance. The latter has to provide the practice teacher with the personal and practical resources to undertake the tasks, and the time and space to do them well. Ill-equipped, unsupported and badly managed practice teachers can foster over-stressed, under-developed and incompetent beginning practitioners. This is not to say that practice teachers are to blame for poor or failing students; many other factors play a part in their emergence. However, the centrality of the practice teacher's role within social work training has to be duly recognised.

The title, "practice teacher", which has superseded that of "student supervisor", is suggestive of a different and developing role. It implies teacher *in the workplace* rather than in the educational setting, with an understanding, between the two settings, of shared aims. The term also implies a more proactive role, as opposed to the reactive term "supervisor" (Thompson, 1991a). Of course, no change of title guarantees a different practice but, without being pedantic, the change of title and its timing is significant. In many ways, the values underpinning the task of the practice teacher are not new and have remained constant: social work education and the profession of social work itself would not have survived thus far without good practice teachers. There has, however, been a catalyst at work which has led to a re-examination of the practice teacher's role.

CCETSW's move towards a three-year qualification for social work resulted in discussion and debate concerning what can be expected of a beginning social worker and how this might be achieved; hence the focus on the role of the practice teacher. Its importance, now defined and clearly stated, has meant that questions of suitability, criteria, training, support and accreditation of practice teachers have to be addressed. Similarly, out of these discussions also emerged the notion of "partnership" between agencies and institutions, employers and educators, with the concept of a joint ownership or responsibility for the emerging social workers. Whether the partners share common goals or the means to achieve them, the partnership has a tendency to converge where theory and practice meet – under the aegis of the practice teacher.

The advent of the Diploma in Social Work (DipSW) and the firming up of proposals for the accreditation of agencies and practice teachers add further weight to the need to be clear about what good practice teaching is and how it can be promoted.

Introduction

Three authors, with different perspectives and agency-specific concerns, combined to put together this work. The triad, when initially formed, represented the very spirit of "partnership", coming from social work education and the field. Membership comprised the university social work teacher, the social services department practitioner and the jointly appointed probation officer/social work lecturer. Initially we three came together to produce working documents focused on practice placements and student evaluation, specifically for the University of Keele CQSW course. In the course of our lengthy and varied deliberations, we trawled for existing structures and frameworks in an effort to make use of the best of these. Elsewhere in the country, no doubt, other "partners" were seeking out ideas or inspiration. We therefore committed this process to print in an effort to offer either a starting point for further deliberation or a structure to work from in your particular partnership. We recognised that other works exist and did not wish to replicate their good efforts. However, given that the area of practice teaching is changing, particularly with CCETSW's greater emphasis on demonstrable and measurable skills, we offered the first edition of this work as our contribution to the continuing debate.

Now, over three years later, further changes in practice teaching have created the need for a second edition – one which builds on the strengths of the first but which also encapsulates new aspects of the practice teaching task. To this effect, we have included an additional chapter which more specifically and explicitly addresses the issues of teaching anti-discriminatory practice. We have also substantially re-written three of the chapters and made amendments to others. One of the new chapters (Chapter 7) addresses the challenge of developing competence-based assessment and explains the philosophy underpinning this approach.

We present this work in a broadly chronological order, moving, as the practice teacher does, from pre-placement planning and arrangements, through to final evaluation. Many of the areas discussed are so central to practice teaching – for example, selection of workload, the role of supervision – that we believe they bear re-examination. Other areas, for example, adult learning, highlight more recently applicable material. Throughout the text many issues pertaining to practice teaching are raised and will be returned to in the concluding section, not to offer any certain solutions but to highlight the need continually to address such issues. Practice teaching cannot be viewed in a vacuum. We must be aware of the need to consider, within the relationship between student, practice teacher and tutor, issues of power, race, gender and so on. Similarly, in specifying 'demonstrable skills' in social work, we have to address the very nature of social work. The ability to collect information and present it to the court in a report, for example, is task-specific but, equally, the values which underpin such action are vital to social work.

Working in the present social and political climate of efficiency, effectiveness and economy – where resources are scarce, individuals and groups are marginalised or ignored and client control is more apparent – the issue of values in social work is central. Additionally, in practice teaching itself, there are many structural and political uncertainties. To work well, practice teaching needs to be adequately resourced and supported. Who is to bear the cost of this and what are the implications for other specialist functions within an agency? If this is to be done through the medium of partnership, how real can the partnership be? These are questions which will need to be addressed.

Practice teaching is developing and changing rapidly. It is in this context that we offer this text to help identify good practice so that it can be incorporated into these new developments.

Chapter 1   considers patterns of adult learning and how these might be applied to the student/practice teacher relationship.

Chapter 2   explores the development of anti-discriminatory practice and offers guidance on how practice teachers can contribute to facilitating learning in this area.

Chapter 3 addresses pre-placement planning and arrangements, from the appropriateness of the placement (matching) to the use of the contract.

Chapter 4 looks at the selection of an appropriate workload, according to the student's learning needs and agency availability.

Chapter 5 takes a critical look at the supervisory relationship, with emphasis on the practicalities and the issues raised.

Chapter 6 considers the various methods by which student performance can be evaluated.

Chapter 7 addresses the complex issue of competence-based assessment.

Chapter 8 is based on a collection of placement scenarios, examples of common problems and how they might be resolved.

We end by asking: 'Why on earth do the job?', and we hope that, in reading this handbook, you will share our optimistic conclusions.

Chapter 1

Patterns of Adult Learning

A practice placement is above all a learning experience geared towards practice-based learning to test, complement and enhance college-based learning. The role of the practice teacher is therefore partly to teach directly and partly to facilitate the student's learning by making appropriate arrangements, such as the allocation of suitable tasks. The student and practice teacher enter into a partnership to take responsibility for the student's learning. The practice teacher is therefore expected to adopt the role of manager – the manager of an educational experience.

An important part of such management is to be able to recognise barriers to learning on the one hand and spurs to learning on the other. In order to facilitate playing this role, the practice teacher needs to develop an understanding of how the student learns, the styles and patterns of learning he/she adopts. What is required, therefore, is a basic understanding of how adults learn in general – the common patterns – and how the student on placement learns in particular.

Adult learning can be seen as significantly different from conventional school-based learning; therefore much of the established literature on education is not applicable. The work of Piaget, for example, relates specifically to the developmental milestones of children's thinking and learning. Our concern is with patterns of adult learning; thus our starting point is very much where Piaget leaves off (see Piaget, 1955).

The behaviourist approach to learning is probably the most familiar to social workers and indeed is the basis for a major approach to social work (Sheldon, 1982). The term 'learning theory' is strongly associated with the behavioural perspective and is in fact more or less synonymous with it. Its main tenets – stimulus-response, reinforcement, and so on – are now so commonplace in social work as to have achieved the (somewhat dubious) status of common sense knowledge. The idea that someone's behaviour is likely to reoccur if it is positively reinforced is now virtually a truism.

There are some serious weaknesses in the behavioural approach (see Chomsky, 1972, and Stevens, 1983, for a critique) but the basic concepts can be of significant value. However, the very ambitious claims of the behaviourists to be able to account for all learning – and indeed for all behaviour – in narrow behavioural terms, display an over-reliance on reinforcements as the be-all and end-all of human learning. Our view of behaviourism, therefore, is not that it is 'wrong' but rather that it makes the mistake of taking one part of a complex pattern and proclaims it to be the whole.

What we have then is a picture of human learning which includes reinforcement (and related concepts) as a very significant but not all-encompassing part. But what are the other parts of this picture?

It is beyond the scope of this handbook to attempt a comprehensive account of adult learning; therefore we shall concentrate on one particular approach which we feel can be of great value to practice teachers.

A number of approaches to learning (as with Piaget, mentioned above) seem to imply that development, and thus learning, stop or at least become far less significant when we attain adulthood. One writer and thinker who, along with his colleagues, definitely does not make this assumption is D A Kolb, who regards learning as an intrinsic and therefore continuous aspect of human experience (Kolb et al, 1971; Kolb, 1984).

Kolb's approach addresses the issue of 'problem-solving', a process he sees as being a key dimension of learning. Learning continues to take place throughout our lives for the simple reason that each day we are faced with new problems to tackle.

Kolb argues that problem-solving can be linked to a process involving four stages and the potential for learning can be enhanced or diminished at each stage. The four stages are:

1. **Concrete Experience**

   This can take a variety of forms. It can be an attempt at formal learning – a book, a lecture, and so on – or more informal opportunities – conversations, day-to-day experiences, and so on. These aspects of concrete experience are the basic building blocks of learning.

2. **Reflective Observation**

   Concrete experience needs to be interpreted – we need to make sense of it. We need to ask the question of what the experience means to us and this question is what characterises the stage of reflective observation. In order to learn from our experiences, we must first reflect upon them and make sense of them.

3. **Abstract Conceptualisation**

   Reflective observation opens the door for a broader and deeper consideration of the issues arising from one's experience. The experience can be linked to other experiences, beliefs and attitudes and thus integrated into one's overall life experience. This entails considering the implications of the concrete experience and evaluating its relevance and validity. Such conceptualisation frequently entails forming a hypothesis or 'working model' of the situation.

4. **Active Experimentation**

   This is the stage at which the hypotheses formed at the previous stage are tested out in practice. The ideas arising from the progression through the three previous stages are now tried out as the learner actively experiments with what he/she has learned.

The first cycle is now complete. However, Kolb's model is not a linear, static one; it is dynamic and continuous, for the end of the first cycle is also the beginning of the second. The active experimentation of one cycle of learning is the basis of the concrete experience stage of the next cycle.

This learning cycle can be illustrated by considering an example from social work practice teaching.

Anne is a DipSW student on placement in a social services office. She is allocated a case in which she is asked to carry out an assessment of the needs of an elderly woman. Reading the referral and discussing the case with her practice teacher form the first concrete experience. She reads and listens carefully and begins to form a picture of what is expected of her. This is her reflective observation. When the supervision session is over and the case is now allocated to her, she begins to form links with the wider areas of knowledge she possesses, including course-based knowledge – the ageing process, the social construction of dependency, client self-determination, and so on. This is the abstract conceptualisation and produces the strategy or set of hypotheses which will guide and inform her active experimentation, that is, the first interview.

This then launches us into the second cycle in which the initial interview provides her with concrete experience. During and immediately after the interview, Anne pieces together and starts to make sense of the experience once again through the process of reflective observation. At this point, Anne feels a bit unsure and confused about her role and the options open to her and to her client. She discusses the case with her practice teacher and this facilitates the abstract conceptualisation. At this stage, understanding can be deepened and extended and contradictions addressed: for example, Anne's realisation of the clash between the client's refusal to accept help and the clearly perceived risk to her health and welfare if existing circumstances were to continue. From this the strategy for the next stage of intervention is developed and the active experimentation stage is set. Anne is now en route for cycle number three, and so on. Each new cycle produces learning which can then play a part in future cycles, for example at the reflection and conceptualisation stages.

Of course, Kolb's model is a simplified version, a snapshot of a complex set of interacting processes. We do not go through one cycle at a time in a neat and orderly fashion but may be going through a number of cycles simultaneously. The model does nonetheless offer a valuable tool for understanding the way adults learn and, equally importantly, the way adults may fail to learn.

In view of this, it is worth devoting our attention to some of the learning hurdles we may fail to jump. This is a particularly important exercise for practice teachers as it offers an insight into the problems of learning which students may encounter on placement. Identifying these problems of learning by reference to the learning cycle can set the scene for tackling such blocks to learning. This exercise may of course also cast light on our own learning strengths and weaknesses as practice teachers. This is a point to which we shall return later.

Problems may occur at the concrete experience stage. If the student avoids taking on work, takes short-cuts (for example, only chatting during an interview instead of tackling the issues) and so on, it is doubtful that learning will take place as the cycle will not have begun.

At stage two, students may not form a sufficiently clear picture of their experience, may misinterpret (for example, not recognise the urgency of a particular referral) or may fail to obtain sufficient or appropriate information.

Abstract conceptualisation is the stage at which the integration of theory and practice is a major issue. The student may eschew conceptualisation perhaps because of an inadequate knowledge-base to draw from or an anti-intellectual rejection of theory in favour of 'getting on with the job'. We cannot learn effectively, argues Kolb, without thinking about our experience and theories give us the conceptual frameworks with which to do this.

In order for learning to be confirmed and consolidated, it is necessary to experiment with it, to put it into practice. Here again students may experience difficulties if they are unwilling or unable to put their ideas into practice. This may be due to not having the courage of one's convictions or it may hinge on excessive caution or shyness. Whatever the underlying reason, this amounts to a significant block to learning.

To be an effective learner it is necessary to be reasonably competent at all four stages. If the student is failing to learn, or at least finding it very difficult, the practice teacher is likely to gain some very significant clues about the remedial steps to take if he/she can identify the stage or stages at which the student struggles. Appropriate assistance can then be offered to boost the student's skills, confidence and capabilities in that area or areas. One point worth noting is that anxiety can be a major stumbling block at any or all of the stages; therefore calming, reassuring and supporting can be a major part of the practice teacher's repertoire.

Kolb extended his analysis of the learning cycle by outlining a set of learning styles, and an exploration of these can also be of value in practice teaching.

Kolb argued that each of us tends to favour one or more particular stages and we develop specific strengths accordingly. This implies that we may be weaker in other areas and may need to devote more attention to these. For example, Anne may be very good at abstract conceptualisation but if she is weak in her reflective observation (for example, by skimping on gathering relevant information) or if she does not put her ideas into action due to a lack of confidence, then her learning potential will be considerably reduced. The practice teacher may then need to assist in the development of assessment skills and information-gathering and/or work on boosting Anne's self-confidence. Targeting the appropriate input from the practice teacher will depend very much on identifying the student's learning style(s).

In order to facilitate this identification, Kolb produced a 'Learning Styles Inventory' (LSI), a questionnaire intended to produce a profile of one's strengths and weaknesses in terms of preferred styles of learning. It is not essential to use the LSI for this purpose as learning styles can be identified through conventional supervisory discussions and examination of work undertaken, and so on. However, the LSI does greatly facilitate this process and has the added advantage of being amenable to self-assessment. That is, practice teachers can use the LSI to further their understanding of their own strengths and weaknesses in learning for, as we wish to stress, supervising a student on placement is both a teaching and a learning experience.

Kolb's model of the learning cycle and learning styles is not as ambitious as behaviourism insofar as it does not attempt to account for all learning. It is one contribution to this area amongst many, but one which can be of particular value in the skills development of social work practitioners, whether students or otherwise.

Kolb's thinking can be used in tandem with our understanding of patterns of adult learning derived from other sources. In order to utilise Kolb's model, we do not need to reject the value of positive reinforcement or the importance of providing an environment conducive to learning, or any other such key aspects of the learning process. In this respect, we have much to gain by making use of Kolb's insights and little or nothing to lose.

Chapter 2

Teaching Anti-Discriminatory Practice

This is one aspect of practice teaching that tends to cause a great deal of anxiety. A common refrain heard on practice teaching courses is that of "They didn't talk about anti-discriminatory practice when I did my training". And indeed there is something of a 'generation gap' insofar as social work theory has moved on considerably in recent years to take on board issues of discrimination and oppression in a way, and to an extent, that was previously unheard of. Consequently, many of today's practice teachers may have had little or no training in anti-discriminatory practice, and yet they are now being asked to act as teachers and facilitators of learning on this very important aspect of modern social work.

It is beyond the scope of this book to introduce practice teachers to the basics of anti-discriminatory practice. For those who feel they need such an introduction, Thompson (1993) is recommended as an introductory text which provides a helpful overview and an account of the main issues. The present focus, therefore, is on teaching anti-discriminatory practice and takes for granted at least a basic understanding of doing anti-discriminatory practice.

CCETSW's Paper 30 states that:

Qualifying social workers must be able to:

- develop an awareness of the inter-relationship of the processes of structural oppression, race, class and gender;

- understand and counteract the impact of stigma and discrimination on grounds of poverty, age, disability and sectarianism;

- demonstrate an awareness of both individual and institutional racism and ways to combat both through anti-racist practice;

15

- develop an understanding of gender issues and demonstrate anti-sexism in social work practice;

- recognise the need for and seek to promote policies and practices which are non-discriminatory and anti-oppressive.

(CCETSW, 1991: p16)

This, then, is the baseline all students must achieve if they are to succeed in obtaining their qualification and becoming qualified social workers. This is also the baseline in terms of establishing this aspect of the practice learning curriculum. It provides a good starting point for addressing issues of teaching anti-discriminatory practice.

What is anti-discriminatory practice?

'Anti-discriminatory practice' is a generic term used to describe an approach to practice which seeks to combat discrimination and oppression. It therefore incorporates anti-racism, anti-sexism, anti-ageism, anti-disablism and so on. It is premised on the recognition that we live in a society in which power and life-chances are unevenly distributed – and this uneven distribution extends to the point where certain groups experience oppression as a result of the disadvantages inherent in the social structure. This oppression manifests itself as racism for members of ethnic minorities, sexism for women and so on. Different forms of oppression can also intertwine and produce double or multiple disadvantages as, for example, in the case of older women experiencing both sexism and ageism.

Social work practice is in a pivotal position in relation to such oppression and disadvantage insofar as social work interventions can either reinforce and amplify the problem or can contribute towards challenging or undermining it. For example, adopting a patronising and paternalistic attitude towards disabled people can add to the marginalisation and discrimination they already experience, whilst adopting an approach based on partnership and empowerment can help to combat and counteract such discrimination:

> There is no comfortable middle ground; intervention either adds to oppression (or at least condones it) or goes some small way towards easing or breaking such oppression. In this respect, the political slogan, 'If you're not part of the solution, you must be part of the problem' is particularly accurate. (Thompson, 1992: p169)

Anti-discriminatory practice is therefore not an 'optional extra', but an essential part of good practice, as the DipSW regulations recognise (CCETSW, 1991). Similarly, teaching anti-discriminatory practice must be seen as an essential part of good educational practice for practice teachers.

Learning strategies

To begin with, it is important to stress that we are using the term 'teaching anti-discriminatory practice' in a fairly loose and generalised way. A more accurate (but rather unwieldy) term would be 'the facilitation of learning how to practise within an anti-discriminatory framework'. The emphasis is not so much on teaching, in the sense of providing knowledge and information, as on the development of skills and a critically self-reflective approach to practice. In order to provide some guidance on facilitating this type of learning, we outline below a number of 'learning strategies' that we feel can be put to good effect in the development of anti-discriminatory and anti-oppressive practice.

• *The hypothetical approach*

It is often argued that issues of racism cannot be covered on certain placements due to the relative absence of black people within a particular geographical area or within the clientele of a particular agency. However, this is not a valid argument, as the development of anti-racist understanding and practice is not premised on the availability of black clients. It is possible to address issues of ethnically sensitive practice and anti-racism by means of a hypothetical approach. That is, a great deal of learning can take place by practice teachers posing hypothetical questions in supervision sessions along the lines of: 'And what if this family were black? What difference would it make?'. The type of discussion which flows from this style of approach can be very useful in helping students understand the need to respond sensitively to the cultural background and needs of service-users, and to recognise the significance of racist oppression.

• *De-individualisation*

One of the common tendencies in social work, firmly rooted in the casework tradition, is that of 'individualisation', the practice of recognising clients as unique individuals. Whilst this clearly has distinct advantages and much to commend it, it also has the

17

disadvantage of discouraging practitioners from seeing clients in their wider social context – specifically within the context of membership of oppressed groups. For example, in dealing with a woman experiencing depression, the significance of gender can be highlighted (Brown and Harris, 1978) and aspects of depression can be related to expectations of female roles in society. In this way, the classic mistake of encouraging women to be more 'feminine' can be avoided. They can be helped to understand their feelings in the context of finding a positive thread of meaning rather than simply slotting into an accepted social role – especially when it may very well be that such oppressive gender expectations played a significant part in the onset of the depression, for example in terms of domestic violence, restricted opportunities for personal fulfilment or sexual abuse. Thus, the process of 'de-individualisation' can be very useful in raising issues of discrimination and oppression and considering constructive ways forward.

- *Block destructive processes*

As anti-discriminatory practice has developed in recent years, a number of destructive processes have also emerged which can act as a barrier to progress. An important role for the practice teacher is to be aware of the potential for such processes developing and, where they begin to do so, use them as a vehicle for exploring the dangers inherent within them. These processes include:

1. *Tokenism:* This amounts to 'going through the motions' by simply making the right sort of noises without actually engaging in anti-discriminatory practice. It often manifests itself in terms of a discrepancy between what is *said* (the use of current jargon) and what is *practised* (traditional forms of practice which, at best, pay only lip service to tackling oppression). Where this arises, it can be a difficult problem to deal with and needs sensitive handling. A balance needs to be found between, on the one hand, not addressing the issue (and thereby colluding with the tokenism) and, on the other, making the student feel so uncomfortable that he or she becomes defensive and avoids engaging with the debate (see the discussion of the Yerkes-Dodson law of adult learning in Chapter 4). There is a significant skill – known as 'elegant challenging' in the context of NLP training (Neuro-Linguistic Programming) – in finding a constructive balance in which the

student feels *challenged* without feeling personally *threatened*. This is an important part of 'perspective transformation', a strategy to be discussed below.

2. *Dogmatism:* Discrimination and oppression are complex matters and it is naive to assume that there can be one simple solution. What can sometimes happen, though, is that one particular approach or strategy comes to be seen as *the* answer, and alternative approaches are dismissed. There is considerable room for debate and we need to be wary of the dogmatic approach which sees, for example, a difference of opinion over a particular anti-racist strategy as a lack of commitment to anti-racism, or even as an example of racism itself. This is a parallel situation to that described by Rojek et al (1988):

> *Like Sedgwick (1982: 237) we hold the view that 'the politicisation of ... problems by radicals and left-wingers is very often of considerable crudity. The [client] tends to be slotted into the general case offered by a certain radical ideology, at the expense of the specifics.' At the same time, we want to defend ourselves from the simple-minded judgement that those who are critical of radical positions must, by that fact, be for traditional forms of theory and practice. (p. 2)*

It is therefore important that we do not allow students to develop such dogmatism, nor should we allow ourselves to impose it upon them through our own views. We need to create an atmosphere of openness and mutual respect. As Rojek et al go on to say: 'Constructive criticism is a valid third option ...' (1988: p2).

3. *Hierarchy of oppressions:* There are various forms of oppression (racism, sexism and so on). One of the fundamental premises of anti-discriminatory practice is the need to tackle oppression in all its forms. One barrier to this is the establishment of a 'hierarchy of oppressions' in which sterile arguments along the lines of 'Sexism is more important than racism' create divisions, tensions and conflicts. It is not unusual for students to take a step in this direction by developing a particular interest in one or more forms of oppression. This, in itself, is not necessarily problematic. However, at times, a student's interest in, and commitment to, a particular form of anti-discriminatory practice may become a

major focus at the expense of other issues. For example, a student may become very interested in anti-ageism and make excellent progress in this area, whilst not getting to grips with important issues of anti-racism and/or anti-sexism and so on. A useful and effective way of tackling such problems is to concentrate on the commonalities of oppression (power, stereotypes and so on) so that learning in one area can be generalised to others. Time can also usefully be spent on exploring the cumulative nature of oppression. For example, black women offenders are over-represented in the criminal justice system (Home Office, 1993: p61), a fact which reflects the compound effects of sexism, racism and the discrimination arising from the stigmatisation of offenders.

4. *Minimisation:* This term describes the tendency to play down the significance of issues of discrimination and oppression, for example by arguing that: 'There aren't many black people around here, so racism isn't really an issue.' This is an attitude which needs to be challenged for three main reasons:

    i) It is *wrong*. The numbers of ethnic minority people are often underestimated in areas where there is no established ethnic minority community.

    ii) It is *irrelevant*. Professional training in social work is intended to equip students to practise effectively throughout the country and not simply within one particular geographical or cultural context.

    iii) It is *racist*. To argue that ethnically sensitive and anti-racist practice is not relevant in predominantly white areas is to argue that the services on offer are tailored primarily to meet the needs of white people – and this clearly has racist implications.

Practice teachers can help students to understand the dangers inherent in 'minimisation' and appreciate how anti-discriminatory practice does not simply apply in inner-city areas.

A further important aspect of this, but one which is not always appreciated, is the significance of racism in working with white clients. For example, in working with white offenders, it may well be the case that there is a racist motivation underlying certain offending incidents, such as criminal damage or assault. A tendency towards 'minimisation' is likely to stand in the way of developing sensitivity to such issues.

5. *Dumping:* Dominelli (1988) makes the point that the responsibility for developing anti-racism must not be 'dumped' on the shoulders of black workers, thereby putting them under pressure to become unofficial race relations experts. Similarly, it is not enough for men to endorse the efforts of women in seeking to establish anti-sexism. *All* social work staff have a responsibility to challenge *all* forms of oppression. We must all take ownership of anti-discriminatory practice and not see it simply as an issue for oppressed groups to tackle for themselves.

- *Perspective transformation*

This is a term used by Mezirow (1981) to refer to a fundamental change in how we perceive the world and our relationship to it. It implies 'unlearning' many of the restrictive patterns of thought into which we have been socialised. In this respect, it is very similar to Freire's (1972) concept of 'conscientization'. Mezirow defines perspective transformation as:

> *the emancipatory process of becoming critically aware of how and why the structure of psycho-cultural assumptions has come to constrain the way we see ourselves and our relationships, reconstituting this structure to permit a more inclusive and discriminating integration of experience and acting upon these new understandings.* It is the learning process by which adults come to recognise their culturally induced dependency roles and relationships and the reasons for them and take action to overcome them. (1981: pp6-7)

This is an important part of anti-discriminatory practice – the development of self-awareness with regard to the effects of the socialisation process upon us in terms of developing stereotypical and potentially oppressive expectations of women, black people, disabled people and so on. Practice teachers can play a significant part in this by seeking out opportunities to encourage and facilitate 'perspective transformation'. An important part of this is the learning strategy that Boud and Walker (1990) call 'noticing':

21

Noticing is an act of becoming aware of what is happening in and around oneself. It is active and seeking, although it may not be formally planned: it involves a continuing effort to be aware of what is taking place in oneself and in the learning experience ... By noticing what is taking place within, the learner may more effectively appreciate what is taking place in the overall situation. External to the learner, it requires attending to the nature of the event and its elements: the forms of interaction between participants, the use of language, cultural patterns, documents and objects used, declared intentions, the continuing change within the event, the presuppositions on which the action of participants are based, the emotional climate of the event and a variety of other things. Noticing acts to feed information from the learning milieu into continuing reflective processes which are integral to the experience and enables the learner to enter into further reflective interaction with it. (p. 68)

Time devoted by practice teachers to identifying and generating opportunities for 'noticing' is therefore likely to be time well spent.

- *Encourage sensitivity to language*

It is important to remember that language not only *reflects* reality but actually *constructs* that reality (Thompson, 1993). That is, the language we use is not neutral or value-free; it has the capacity either to reinforce discrimination or to challenge it. Helping students develop sensitivity to language is therefore an important strategy in developing anti-discriminatory practice. In particular, there are four types of language use that can prove problematic. These are:

1. *Exclusion:* Certain language forms exclude women and contribute to their 'invisibility' in society. Terms such as 'chair*man*' or '*man*power' not only reflect male dominance but also reinforce that dominance by creating the impression that positions of power are reserved for men.

2. *Dehumanisation:* Language can also have the effect of treating people as if they were things by the use of depersonalising terms such as 'the disabled' (rather than disabled *people)* or 'the elderly' (rather than older *people).*

3. *Infantilisation*: This refers to the tendency to treat adults as if they were children. Women, for example, are often referred to as girls ('the office girls'), and other groups of people (older people and people with learning disabilities, for example) are also often referred to in child-like terms – a tendency which has the effect of patronising the people concerned.

4. *Stigmatisation:* Some language forms create or reinforce negative images and therefore result in some people being stigmatised. For example, the term 'black' is often used in a negative and derogatory way (a 'black' day, a 'black' mark) or in the sense of 'dirty' ('black' knees).

In tackling issues of language with students, it is important to remember that the focus is on learning. That is, the issues need to be addressed in a constructive educational way, rather than a punitive way. If students become defensive, it is unlikely that they will be able to develop the sensitivity to language required. At best, they will mechanistically learn which terms are frowned upon but without understanding why these are best avoided.

- *learn together*

Developing anti-discriminatory practice is a difficult and demanding process which can be painful and distressing at times, especially as this process often involves 'letting go' of previously held values and unlearning previous patterns of socialisation. It is therefore essential that we work together and support each other through these difficulties. Central to this endeavour is the recognition that there are no 'experts' if, by expert, we mean someone who has all the answers. It is not simply a matter of the enlightened casting pearls of wisdom before the unenlightened. In this respect, as in many other aspects of social work, we can learn from students as well as teach them. In developing anti-discriminatory practice, we are swimming against the tide of power structures and dominant ideological forces, and so it is likely that the struggle against discrimination and oppression will be a life-long one. This is all the more reason why we should learn together.

Conclusion

DipSW students face a considerable challenge in meeting the requirements of anti-discriminatory practice. Understanding the theory base is the first step, but actually putting that theory into practice is the much more difficult challenge. And this is where the practice teacher comes in – by playing an active part in that process of applying theory to practice, in this case applying anti-discriminatory theory to practice.

As we have seen, there are no simple, 'formula' solutions that we can bring to bear, no straightforward means of developing anti-discriminatory practice. We are all part of a long-term process and we all still have a lot to learn on the way. One way we can facilitate this process is by sharing our learning and creating a supportive and constructive atmosphere of mutual trust and co-operation. This is particularly important in order to prevent the inherent political tensions from overspilling and creating a destructive atmosphere based on infighting and defensiveness, rather than one of collaboration as part of an anti-oppressive alliance.

We hope that this chapter will help you in fulfilling your duties as a practice teacher with regard to anti-discriminatory practice. However, what is also important is that we take forward our learning into other aspects of practice teaching so that anti-discriminatory practice becomes integrated within the overall learning and practice ethos, rather than simply a discrete aspect of it. It is vital, therefore, that, at every stage of your learning about practice teaching, you relate the issues under consideration to the framework of anti-discriminatory practice. That is, other aspects of learning need to be seen in the context of discrimination and oppression and the humanitarian duty to counter them.

Chapter 3

Pre-placement Planning

It is possible to identify four stages in the process of setting up a placement, in three of which the practice teacher is actively involved. The model described is not rigid in prescription; the process may vary with, for example, the degree of prior collaboration between course and agency, or the procedures within agencies for the allocation and organisation of placements. However, we believe that it reflects current good practice in a wide range of colleges and agencies, and we further believe that all these stages must, in one way or another, be methodically worked through if a satisfactory learning experience is to follow. To skimp on preparatory work is to set the placement at hazard; it may succeed (and may have succeeded) despite shortcomings in prior planning – but success in these circumstances is likely to depend upon a combination of improvisation and good luck. Improvisation may at times be a virtue, but it has its limitations; reliance upon good luck is no part of competent professional practice in either education or social work.

1. The Placement Request

The search for the placement begins in the college, in the minds of student and tutor and in developing dialogue between them. It is far too simple to assume on the one hand that the student's wishes are predominant, or on the other that he/she will simply fit in with what is convenient. Nor is it in any way adequate for a college to forward details of a student which consist merely of a brief curriculum vitae, followed by some such statement as 'wishes to experience work in a child guidance setting'.

Characteristically, students will have ideas derived from their own or others' experience and will frequently frame these in terms of preference for a particular setting or client group. They are also likely to be influenced by practical issues such as travelling time or convenience to home. The tutor, on the other hand, is more likely to define placement needs in relation to some implicit concept of a practice curriculum – to stages of skill development, acceptance of responsibility, strengthening of identified areas of weakness.

Tutors, too, have their practical imperatives – the need to support a student unit, or to encourage a particular agency and, of course, the limitations of available experience. Between the two of them, they must refine their ideas into a coherent and realistic specification of the experience sought; this can only be achieved by constructive dialogue and, to have any real value, the resulting statement must be a joint venture (even if it will occasionally reflect differences of view).

Considerable responsibility for initiating and maintaining this process falls on the tutor: it is the tutor, not the student, who has expertise in social work education, who should be able to help the student identify his/her professional learning needs as opposed to personal preferences, who should have sufficient knowledge (in general terms at least) of what the available placement may offer. The tutor may, for example, have to destroy popular fallacies (that probation is all about control, not about helping; that work with older people is just a matter of arranging services) or ascertain the limits of prior experience (whether three years in a social services department taught the student to assess need and plan intervention, or just to carry out agency procedures) or explain the potential and limitations of various agencies (that family therapy is practised in the probation civil team as well as in the child guidance clinic). He/she may also need to make clear to the student that the placement represents not just a chance to widen experience, but an assessed part of the course in which achievement in social work tasks will be examined and evaluated.

In framing the final request, we find it helpful to think in terms of two components. First is a general curriculum, which relates to expectations of tasks to be completed and standards to be achieved at any given stage of the course, and is therefore applicable to any student. This might, for example, include an expectation that all first placement students will proceed from simple data-gathering to analytic assessment and planned intervention, or that they may be expected to negotiate on the agency's behalf in routine matters relating to their own clients. The second component is personal to the particular student, consisting of work which may require special emphasis. For example, one student might need close and supportive supervision to overcome uncertainty deriving from previous experience, while a second might anticipate problems in exercising authority.

This point may be illustrated by two students undertaking final probation placements in the same training unit. Part of the specification was identical for both – the need to demonstrate competence as a beginning probation officer and beginning social worker. One, however, had limited experience of the probation service and would need her placement directing towards its procedures and practice and her new identity within it. The other was much more familiar with probation and it was possible to identify her need to complement prior experience of young male offenders with work with older men and with women; moreover, as there was some ground for thinking that her practical skills ran ahead of her grasp of theoretical material, concentration upon this was specified as an important element.

Information on the student needs to be parallelled by information about the course, and this can be a difficult area; a massive collection of syllabuses may not be very informative and, anyway, reflects what the staff teach (or say they teach!) rather than what the student learns. Nevertheless, a responsibility rests with the tutor to ensure (probably by some form of written information at this stage, supplemented later by the student's own perception of what has been learned) that the agency has some understanding of where the placement comes in the overall pattern of learning. Every social work course has its own structure and every one probably thinks its own is best. The one undeniable fact is that every student arrives on placement with gaps in learning; the nature of the gaps varies with the course he/she comes from. If the practice teachers are to be seen as colleagues, it is essential that they are fully informed of the educational structure, a significant part of which is their responsibility.

The end product of this process of dialogue and refinement of ideas will be a written request to the agency for a placement. The format will vary from course to course; the example provided in Appendix 1 will serve to illustrate the main points. These will include (part 1 of the example) basic factual data to provide some sort of profile of the individual, and of his/her educational, work and life experience, and (part 2 of the example) an outline of the placement expectation. Practical issues, such as availability of transport or family commitments which might have a bearing on the viability of the placement, must also be included at this stage. Finally, we would draw attention (part 3 of the example) to the desirability of seeking reciprocal information on agency and practice teacher; it is a frequent and frustrating experience for students to find that, while the practice teachers have been well informed about them, they know nothing of these people who are to be so important in their lives.

2. The Decision in Principle

It may well be that a decision in principle has been taken before the request ever arrives: that one team is too busy to accommodate students this year, or that a newly-trained practice teacher should take a student as soon as possible. Even without such clear-cut examples, however, there is work to be done in the agency in advance of the requests arriving. What is the attitude of managers and practitioners towards student placements? Is there a policy of favouring a particular course or a particular group of students? Are there some areas of work deemed inappropriate? Who will be available to take students if requested, and what back-up can they expect? Quite simply, a manager with a modicum of foresight will anticipate these and other questions, rather than improvising when the requests arrive. Practice teachers have a duty (quite apart from self-interest) to ensure that their agencies formulate and periodically review policy on placements along with other aspects of their work.

As with courses, agencies differ in the ways in which they handle placement requests: sometimes it falls to training staff, sometimes to district managers or team leaders to identify appropriate practice teachers. Whoever does the job, its importance should not be underestimated, for it is often in the agency rather than in college that the matching of student to practice teacher takes place. Tutors will, of course, frequently ask for, and often be given, a known and tried colleague – but with increased job mobility in social work, combined with the fact that practice teachers are, by definition, experienced workers who are likely to seek promotion, this "old pals network" becomes less reliable than it once was. This may be illustrated by the fact

28

that a tutor with nearly twenty years experience in one centre found that he had previously worked with only two out of thirty practice teachers taking first year students from his course.

Assuming that a given practice teacher has been identified by the agency and approached to take a particular student, he/she must ask two questions – can I take any student, and can I take this student? The answer to the first will depend upon factors such as workload, accommodation and team support; to the second, upon consideration of the specification provided by the college. It is worth making an important point here: if the information received is inadequate, the practice teacher has a right, and arguably a duty, to ask for amplification. As a general rule, it can be assumed that practice teachers are operating in a seller's market; the demand for placements gives them considerable power *vis-a-vis* the colleges, and it is surprising how few use this power to extract the levels of service to which they are entitled.

Neither of these questions can be answered by the practice teacher alone; both require consultation with team members, managers and other colleagues. This may seem self-evident in relation to the general question of practicability, but it is also true of the second, of particular student need. If the student needs experience of, say, a client group with whom the practice teacher does not deal, may cases be borrowed from another team? Will it be necessary to enlist the help of specialist colleagues (court officers perhaps, or advisers on ethnic groupings) to provide the necessary opportunities? There are now very few settings, if any, in which the practice teacher can offer a successful placement on the basis of being sole instructor, and the role is increasingly (as will be seen in subsequent sections) one of manager of an educational experience.

Two contrasting examples illustrate the importance of ensuring that the environment is appropriate for the student. Liz, a second year DipSW student, arrived at her second placement showing puzzling apprehension at joining the team. It transpired that her first experience had been an unhappy one because her practice teacher had been the only member of his team who wanted a student and Liz, while receiving very helpful instruction from him, had been largely ostracised by his colleagues. Remi, on the other hand, was a student destined for probation but taking an early placement in a social services department. Very much wanting experience with children and families, he found that a late failure in arrangements necessitated him being placed in a team dealing with elderly people. An office with a helpful and positive attitude rallied around him and his practice teacher; cases were 'loaned' and resources pooled to provide a very broadly-based experience which matched his needs well.

It might appear (and certainly often does to the students) that, if the answers to both the earlier questions are in the affirmative, the search is at an end, the placement is fixed and there is no more to it. At this stage, though, the decision can only be in principle. However good the information flow, however careful the agency assessment, it is not possible to confirm the placement until the three parties – student, tutor and practice teacher – have met, added flesh to the bones of the written material and agreed a contract.

3. The Learning Agreement

Typically, the learning agreement or placement contract will be drawn up at a pre-placement visit by tutor and student to the host agency; we choose to describe this meeting as the 'contract visit' to emphasise its focus. Whether a written document is produced at this stage or later is a matter for discretion, some workers taking the view that its final form is best fixed a week or so into the placement after practice teacher and student have had more chance to find out their respective needs, interests and offerings. Whichever approach is adopted, it is essential that a clear written statement, agreed by all three parties, is in existence at the start of the placement or, at latest, two weeks into it.

The purpose of the learning agreement is to establish, unambiguously, the aims of the placement, the means whereby they will be achieved and the rights and responsibilities of the three parties to it. It provides a baseline from which the progress of the placement may be judged and to which reference will be made from time to time to ensure that the work is proceeding according to schedule. It cannot be an absolutely rigid blueprint, since flexibility is needed to adapt to changes in working environment and in pace for student learning – but it needs to provide for changes in direction and emphasis to be recorded so that the new track of the placement may be accurately plotted.

The value of a learning agreement in helping the practice teacher plan and run the placement may, ironically, be illustrated by a worker operating to a verbal agreement before written contracts became popular. At the end of a very happy and productive placement, a student said: 'We always seemed to be laughing and enjoying ourselves a lot but, in the last three weeks as we began to wind up the work, I suddenly realised that we had done everything which, at the beginning of the placement, he had said we would do'. This was an example of a skilled practice teacher working to a carefully constructed plan and retaining control of the placement process; to have control of the process is to demonstrate professional skill in practice teaching, and the contract may well be the most important single step in gaining control.

The production of the contract involves the fusion of the two earlier stages of preparatory work: tutor and student bring to the contract meeting their ideas and their agenda, formulated at the request stage; the practice teacher arrives with all the factors considered in making the decision in principle; a process of exploration, exchange and negotiation then results in agreement upon a viable arrangement, summarised in the contract.

It is important for future relationships (as well as being a potentially valuable learning experience for the student) that the negotiations are conducted at a level of professional discussion rather than casual exchange. This is not to say they should be cold and unfriendly – the three will need to work closely together in the months ahead. Still less can they be insensitive – students at least will have a high anxiety level, and the problems of knowing where to park the car or what clothes to wear may loom larger than the theoretical orientation of the practice teacher. But each party must be able to state with some confidence his/her minimal needs and realistic contribution, must be able to move beyond initial reactions of like or dislike to a more objective assessment of the potential for collaboration, and must, in short, be able to engage in the process of inter-professional negotiation which will play such an important part in much of the student's future day-to-day social work practice.

In this process of negotiation, it may be that some desired objectives cannot be guaranteed, or even offered; other options of which student and tutor were unaware when they requested the placement may materialise. Thus, for example, it may be unlikely, given the flow of work to the agency at this time, that a student will be able to pick up and carry through to conclusion a fostering application – but this may be offset by unanticipated opportunities for groupwork practice with existing fostering applicants. As with any negotiation process, the parties must decide what is the acceptable bottom line, what can be sacrificed in the interests of achieving another more important aim, just when an acceptable level of agreement has been reached.

In reality, tutor and practice teacher have to take much of the responsibility for this negotiation. This is not to say that the student has no voice; on the contrary, the student is at the centre of the whole process and his/her opinions must be sought. However, given the characteristic shortage of practice placements and the consequent level of anxiety surrounding them, it takes a good deal of nerve, courage and confidence for a student to say no. The more experienced parties to the negotiation, (particularly the tutor, who has a direct responsibility for the student's overall development) may need to help him/her to do so. In that case, it is the duty of the tutor to support the student as the search for an alternative begins; the practice teacher's responsibility lies in assisting the decision not to make a contract on this occasion.

We would feel that the tutor plays a central role in the learning agreement negotiation, as the initiator of the process and the bearer of responsibility for the student's course experience, and is therefore the member of the triad who should sum up the discussion, confirm understanding by all parties and conclude by explicitly asking that agreement has been reached. A simple formula such as: 'So we have a placement then?', signals that the negotiation has been successfully pursued and that a contract may be agreed and signed.

4. Preparing the Ground

Once the placement has been confirmed and the contract made, the practice teacher must begin to tie up the numerous loose ends which will inevitably be left from earlier stages of preparation and make the detailed arrangements necessary for the student's arrival. In an ideal world, there would be ample time for them; in reality, the practice teacher may well have to work quickly to offset the disadvantage of an approach which comes late in the day.

Perhaps the first question which springs to mind is that of choice and availability of work for the student – something which is so fundamental that we discuss it in a separate chapter. There are, however, more mundane issues to be dealt with: Where will he/she sit? Is there a desk available? Can arrangements be made for use of official car parking? and so on. In a sense, the practice teacher needs to step outside the agency, see it from the student's viewpoint, and identify all these minor facts of life within it which may be strange or disconcerting to the outsider.

There is, too, the very important area of preparing colleagues for the student's arrival. This is particularly relevant in the case of those who will be directly and closely involved with his/her work: the specialist workers (court officer, perhaps welfare rights worker) who will contribute directly to teaching; the clerical staff who may be asked to undertake extra work or explain filing systems. However, since a new (and probably rather inquisitive but slightly apprehensive) colleague will be joining the agency on a temporary basis, it is desirable that all staff know of his/her arrival, and something too about background experience.

An additional use of preparation is likely to be what may be termed official procedures. In most agencies, the question of police clearance will arise (and the pattern and time-scale of obtaining these appears so variable that we would hesitate to generalise: find out agency practice, and put it into operation as soon as possible seems the best advice). Identification of some form is likely to be needed; some agencies require medical clearance; if the student is to use a car, insurance cover will need to be checked. Personal safety is perhaps too important to be relegated to *official procedures* – but the agency should have systems marked out for issue of personal alarms, ensuring there is no risk of leaving isolated buildings alone at night, and so on; it is the practice teacher's duty to ensure that the student is included from the first day in the working of these systems.

Finally there is the element of personal preparation: gearing myself up for the student. This will imply planning the course of the placement (probably on paper: the discipline is useful, and it serves as a permanent *aide-memoire*), anticipating what needs to be done by whom, and when, and how to do it. It may, though, also mean undertaking preliminary reading, a short revision course in social work theory. New practice teachers are at least two years away from their own training; some material learned in this training will be in daily use, some will not (and it is on this which the student may well seek guidance!). This is not to say that the practice teacher is meant to be a high-flying academic or a full-time theorist; but if he/she says to the student, 'I use a task-centred approach' or 'This agency specialises in crisis intervention', the student may reasonably expect a coherent explanation of the ideas underlying the practice. Very often, using and modifying ideas from day to day, we move away from the source material and are rarely confronted with the need to elaborate it. The arrival of the student changes that – which is one of the stimuli of practice teaching.

It is possible to construct a checklist of pre-course action, which might include arranging workload, informing and enlisting colleagues, obtaining necessary clearances and documentation, making practical arrangements for accommodation for the student, undertaking preparatory reading and planning. However, we would suggest that it is better for the agency's training section, in conjunction with its practice teachers, to have a standard list to assist staff who are planning to take students, rather than leaving individuals to re-invent the wheel. If a new practice teacher finds such a list is not available, he/she might well take the initiative in asking for one to be constructed.

Chapter 4

Selection of Workload

One of the key skills practice teachers need to develop is that of setting the student's workload at a reasonable and realistic level. There are a number of dimensions to this issue and getting it right involves a complicated juggling and balancing act. The aim of this chapter is to explore these dimensions and begin to piece together an overall picture of workload selection.

It is a common complaint from students that the amount of work expected of them during their placements is set at an inappropriate level. Where this occurs, the imbalance usually seems to be in the direction of insufficient work, and this parallels the common anxiety of practice teachers about the dangers of overloading students. How then do we establish the balance between being underworked and overworked?

The first step towards this is to consider the overall workload in terms of its component parts. In fieldwork placements it is common practice to think in terms of 'caseload' but this is misleading as it distracts attention from other aspects of the workload, such as visits of observation, attendance at meetings, case conferences and so on, observed or joint work, specific projects or fact-finding missions (for example, to draw up a list of services for older people to act as the basis of an information leaflet), duty work, and so on. Also, the over-reliance on the term 'caseload' can be seen to marginalise residential, day care and community work placements by devaluing work other than cases.

Having taken an overall perspective of the student's possible workload, the guiding principle for deciding how much of each is appropriate for the student should be that of learning needs. One of the major tasks for the practice teacher is to seek to match learning opportunities to the learning needs identified at the contract stage. This is a good example of the role of the practice teacher as the 'manager' of a learning experience. Part of this management role is to ensure that a suitable range of learning experiences is made available and this may entail considerable conflict in the following ways:

- between the student's wishes and his/her perceived needs;
- between the tutor's perceptions of the needs and those of the practice teacher;
- between the needs identified and the opportunities for meeting them available during the placement.

The first two will hopefully have been resolved in the contract discussions but may re-emerge during the placement. The third potential conflict is one which will need to be managed and monitored as the placement progresses – and here some 'compensation' between the areas of workload may be needed.

The practice teacher may need to seek out appropriate learning experiences by 'borrowing' work from other teams or work settings. This sort of 'cross-fertilisation' can of course be beneficial for both the student in particular and the work setting in general. It also has the added advantage of moving us away from the preciousness of some practice teachers about 'my' student.

Since the student's learning needs are, of course, the primary focus, it is worth considering them in more detail before moving on to consider other aspects of workload.

Learning needs come in a variety of shapes and sizes, but most, if not all, fall within one or more of the following four broad categories:-

1. *Applying Theory to Practice*

   The opportunity to use a particular method (for example, implementing a behaviour modification programme) or to work within a particular theoretical framework (for example, crisis intervention).

2. *Practice Learning*

   The development of practice skills, such as interviewing, recording and effective communication.

3. *Procedural Learning*

Agency-specific learning of administrative and procedural processes, such as child protection procedures, court procedures, and so on.

4. *Emotional Learning*

Recognising, responding to, and coming to terms with the emotional effects of intervention and the implications for the worker's own feelings.

How much work to allocate to the student will depend largely on the relative balance of these needs. A student who is very competent in one of these aspects of learning will be able to get through considerably more work of that type than a student who struggles in that particular area. It is therefore important to get to know the student, to know which are his/her major learning needs and which minor. This will be a key factor in determining how much work needs to be done in each of the areas and this in turn provides important guidance as to the appropriate overall workload. There is of course no simple or clear-cut formula which can be applied to calculate the amount of work to be allocated. Judging the level of work is a major part of the management role of the practice teacher and therefore needs to be monitored and reviewed.

A further important dimension which needs to be considered is how comfortable the student should be with his/her work. There is a continuum between feeling totally confident and at ease with one's work at one end, and panicking, losing control and being overwhelmed at the other. The significant point to note about this continuum is that each of the two extremes minimises learning. Feeling too comfortable can lead to complacency and this in turn can lead us to miss important learning points or opportunities to develop. Learning necessarily involves a degree of discomfort, as it entails a slight readjustment of one's knowledge base and perhaps a challenge to things we have previously taken for granted. At the other extreme, excessive anxiety can be a significant block to learning, as we are more likely to invest our energies in surviving a very stressful situation, rather than making maximum use of the learning opportunities available. However, having said this, it must be remembered that crises can also be major sources of learning, as our problem-solving capacities can be stretched to the full. (This is, of course, the basis of Crisis Intervention Theory – see Caplan, 1961; Thompson, 1991b). Nonetheless, the use of crisis as a learning tool needs to be carefully managed and supervised as it is unfair, unhelpful and potentially destructive to expose a student to crises without adequate support and guidance.

The middle ground of this continuum is therefore the strongest basis for facilitating learning as it offers a balance, providing confidence and a relaxed manner on the one hand and a degree of stretching and challenge on the other. Research studies have shown that adults learn most effectively when motivation and anxiety (or 'affectivity') are moderate, neither too high nor too low. This has become known as the 'Yerkes-Dodson Law' of learning (see Cropley, 1977: p96). Again, the practice teacher's judgement in achieving this balance will be a central issue and another example of a management skill expected of good practice teachers. The selection of workload should therefore reflect this judgement.

The level, type and amount of work deemed appropriate for a student will of course depend on the stage in the course at which the placement falls – that is, introductory, intermediate or final. The structure of courses varies to a certain extent. However, each contains an introductory and a final placement, with some also having an intermediate developmental placement.

It is not possible to provide a formula or precise set of rules to govern the matching of work tasks to level of placement, but there are, nonetheless, broad guidelines which can assist us in making a success of this matching process.

In the first assessed placement the focus is on generic skills. This is not to say that the placement should be generic – generic teams appear to be becoming increasingly rare – but the skills, knowledge and values addressed should none the less be generic in the sense of being common across social work settings. That is, regardless of the placement setting, the common basis of social work practice should be to the fore – communication skills, planning and assessment skills, anti-discriminatory practice and so on.

For the final assessed placement, the focus is on the 'area of particular practice' (APP), that is, the student's chosen area of specialism. In this placement the generic skills of social work continue to play an important part, as indeed they do for any social work practice. However, at this stage in the student's development, there is an additional set of issues to be addressed – the knowledge, skills and values relevant to the APP chosen. For example, in choosing older people as an APP, a student is committing him/herself to addressing issues which are specific to older people. This would include, amongst other things, developing competence not only in the generic skills of assessment, but also the specific skills of carrying out an assessment with an older person, for example, the ability to work within an anti-ageist framework. Similarly, in child care, a first placement student working with a child care team would need to understand only the basic principles, requirements and implications of the Children Act 1989. However, a second placement student would be expected to have a much more detailed grasp of the legislative base and thus be able to work at a more advanced level.

These guidelines can be used for reference when allocation of work is under consideration and will, of course, also be useful and relevant when assessment of the student's performance is to the fore (see Chapters 6 and 7), as they can be a good indication, broadly speaking, of what level of development the student should have attained.

Where an intermediate placement is available, this tends to act as a bridge between the introductory and final placements; the level and amount of work chosen should reflect, as far as possible, this 'bridging' or intermediate status. It is also an excellent opportunity for students to try out new ideas or undertake a wider variety of tasks without the pressure of assessment inhibiting them. It is therefore an opportunity to break new ground and take whatever steps one can to maximise learning – providing, of course, that such learning is not at the client's expense.

There are some other issues relating to the selection of workload which are likely to arise.

One common problem which needs to be avoided is the 'extra pair of hands' syndrome. It is very tempting, especially in a highly pressurised work-setting, to use a student as a means of taking pressure off colleagues. Where this occurs, a number of problems are created. There is risk of the student being overworked and thus learning bad habits by cutting corners or skimping, rather than having the space to learn time-management skills which are necessary for coping with high levels of pressure. Also, the selection of workload would tend to be geared towards the needs of the hard-pressed agency rather than to the learning needs of the student. This could prove disastrous, not only for the student but also for the agency, as the student may be ill-equipped to act as an extra pair of hands in this way.

Another key aspect of workload selection is the student's development of a professional identity as a social worker. The moral-political context of the social work enterprise is one which needs to be addressed as part of professional development – a critical examination of aims and values. Here the significant dimensions of class, race, gender, age and disability will play an important role. The selection of workload will need to pay attention to the opportunities afforded for the development of anti-discriminatory practice. If a real integration of the theoretical and practical elements is to be achieved, the moral-political context of aims and values needs to be reflected, as far as possible, in the placement workload and not restricted to an academic discussion within the college/university setting.

One final issue worthy of note is the tension between variety and consolidation. A balance needs to be struck between variety – a wide range of learning opportunities – on the one hand and consolidation – a number of similar learning opportunities which offer depth rather than breadth of learning – on the other. Once again there can be no formula to apply to this; it rests as a management responsibility for the practice teacher to judge the appropriate balance of breadth and depth, of variety and consolidation.

In summary, this chapter has presented the case for workload selection to be geared towards:-

1. the learning needs of the student as identified partly at the contract stage and partly as the placement progresses;

2. a balance between the student being stretched or challenged and being comfortable and confident;

3. the stage of the course at which the placement falls and the differential expectations of student performance accordingly;

4. maximum learning benefit for the student rather than maximum staffing benefit for the agency;

5. the development of professional identity in terms of aims, values and anti-discriminatory practice;

6. a balance between breadth and depth of learning.

All of these factors will, of course, be underpinned by the individual experience, strengths and weaknesses of the particular student, not to mention the relationship which develops between student and practice teacher. Taking account of such a range of factors and coming up with a successful matching of workload to student need is by no means a simple or easy task and, as we have emphasised, there can be no straightforward formula to be applied. What is required is the capacity to make a series of considered and balanced judgements for, as we have seen, the role of practice teacher is a management role which entails the fostering of such skills as assessing need, promoting and evaluating strategies to meet need and taking responsibility for this process – skills already familiar to experienced social workers.

Chapter 5

The Supervisory Process

We have already acknowledged the relevance of the change of title from student supervisor to practice teacher. It is therefore somewhat paradoxical that the student is still generally said to be 'supervised' by the practice teacher. The Oxford English dictionary defines supervision as "having the oversight of ... superintending the execution or performance of the movements or work of a person". To supervise is to: "look over, survey, inspect, read through, peruse and revise". The term does not therefore do justice to the practice teacher who, in addition to all the above, also works to enable or facilitate the student's learning, and in the course of the supervisory process, will also engage in some direct teaching. Each of these aspects does not detract from the supervisory role: the practice teacher has a dual responsibility – to the student and to his/her agency, and, through the latter, an accountability to the client(s) with whom the student is working.

Practice teachers need to be clear what supervision means, in theory and reality. We all tend to carry around some notion of supervision in practice, and often this is informed by bad or poor personal experience of being supervised. However, whether a student or an experienced social work practitioner, there is nothing as valuable or energising as good supervision. But what is good supervision? How is it achieved? We will consider these questions by reviewing the content of student supervision and its process, as these are key aspects of effective practice teaching.

Just as the previous discussion on adult learning pointed to the relevance of our early experiences of teaching and learning, so we must also take this into account when considering the supervision relationship. Students may come to supervision with expectations of lively debate and critical analyses of working practices; others will expect to be examined on their work and gently led into new arenas. Some students, perhaps because of previous teaching environments or a total lack of such experience, act as an empty vessel into which knowledge, in the shape of 'the right answers', will be poured by the all-knowing practice teacher. Equally, as practice teachers, we have to acknowledge our experiences of the teaching role, which can be a very powerful one. How do we control this power – do we retain it as the expert practitioner who instructs the student, rationing such knowledge according to our assessment of the student's needs? Do we share our power by empowering the student to have the confidence and competence to practise? And how is this done – do we protect students until we gauge the moment for them to face difficult issues or practice? Should we 'throw them in at the deep end' to get some measure of existing skills and abilities? Or do we subscribe to the apprenticeship model of social work learning?

These examples may seem somewhat extreme and perhaps we all use a mixture of approaches. What we need to be clear about, however, is why we use the different techniques and whether these meet our needs as practice teachers or the students' learning needs. There is no one correct methodology. What we have to do is examine our attitudes, motives and personal style. Similarly, we should examine the relevance of gender and race to our relationship as practice teacher and student. To ignore each aspect is to discount the importance of previous and present life experiences and the power dimension in the supervisory relationship. While many of these aspects will need to be acknowledged and discussed between practice teacher and student (and tutor) there will have to be a preliminary self-examination. To undertake this process calls for good supervision from our line managers or peer group practice teachers acting in a consultancy role, or indeed the assistance of a consultant to the placement.

The Purpose of Supervision

While previous authors have made useful contributions to the discussions about supervision (see, for example, Butler and Elliot, 1985; Brown, 1984; Morrison, 1993) the key principles are worth summarising:

1. Supervision ensures that client and agency needs are being met. As practitioners, students have to be accountable to both.

2. Supervision assesses and evaluates the students' learning needs and their ability to practise.

3. Supervision informs the students' practice.

Good supervision should also:

4. Stretch the students' creative and critical abilities and test them in practice;

5. Consciously integrate the students' theoretical understanding with social work practice;

6. Enhance the students' knowledge and understanding of wider social work, structural and value issues.

The Practicalities of Supervision

There are numerous ways in which supervision can take place. Clearly, any aspect of a student's practice which is open to observation is also open to scrutiny and could therefore be open to supervision. The nature and size of an agency will have a bearing on the practicalities of supervision and it is important to make use of a flexible approach which capitalises on the opportunities provided by the agency setting. None of these factors should detract however from the student's right to *planned, protected* and *purposeful* supervision.

These will obviously have to take account of agency constraints. For example, while it might be possible to identify the same afternoon each week for the normal supervision session within a field team setting, this might be impossible in the residential setting when faced with complex staff duty rotas. However, in principle, the learning needs of the student are of paramount importance except where these conflict with the rights and needs of clients or the policy of the agency. Two missed supervision sessions should alert the practice teacher to the need to reassess the arrangements. Such arrangements should be specified at the pre-placement meeting and therefore open to regular review.

Although it is important that time should be available for informal consultation, regular timetabled supervision sessions are necessary. Supervision sessions should be for a minimum of one and a half hours per week unless circumstances are exceptional. To ensure an uninterrupted period away from work pressures, the supervision session should be free from telephone or personal calls on the practice teacher's and student's time.

The degree of informal supervision given to the student can depend on personal preference; some practice teachers have an 'open door' system, while others make positive use of colleagues to widen the student's experience. Whether these approaches are appropriate will depend on the student's use of them; very regular informal supervision may be appropriate for the beginning student but would raise questions if it persisted to the same extent at final placement stage. Similarly, the use of colleagues in addition to the practice teacher can be a healthy sign, but could also indicate a student's search for like-minded others when there is a difference of opinion between student and practice teacher.

Supervision should be a dynamic experience, which not only meets student needs but is part of the practice teacher's continuing learning. The student should be expected to contribute to the process of supervision by setting agendas for the sessions with the practice teacher. Preparation for the sessions, for example, specific reading, data collection, or written records, is important for both student and practice teacher.

Practice teacher and student should keep notes of supervision sessions, whether jointly or separately. Some agencies have proforma one-page supervision records which can be filled in succinctly. The recording of supervision sessions is a means of charting student learning, areas of movement, issues or disagreements, the focus of future learning, task-setting and so on. The audio or video recording of supervision sessions can also provide the means for the practice teacher to be supervised or for material for the course tutor to use as consultant to the duo. In terms of the practice teacher's own development, notes of previous students' supervision sessions can provide a useful basis for comparing students' varying stages of development.

The role of the tutor in the supervisory relationship is generally not an active one; rather the tutor provides a broader perspective of the relationship as it is related by practice teacher and student, or on the basis of written, audio or video recording of supervision. As such, the involvement of the tutor remains at a distance and this has its advantages when the tutor's intervention can provide overview of the placement experience. This can be particularly helpful when there are problems in the placement and the tutor is able to provide an external measure relevant to the stage of the student's learning, or based on his/her knowledge of the student's work in the educational setting. There may be a role for the tutor to be directly involved in the supervisory relationship as a live consultant, probably occurring when practice teacher, student or tutor are concerned about some element of practice or professional relationship. The tutorial visit can be useful not only to inspect progress but also as an aid to supervision. It is important, however, that the functions and parameters of the tutor's role are clear to all concerned.

Programmes/courses use tutors from a variety of sources, some programme teachers, others recruited specifically for the tutorial role; some as joint appointees with an interest and experience in both settings, others who are historically departmental members but whose first allegiance lies with the broader academic world. Student and practice teachers can therefore expect a variable service from the tutor whose perception of their role may also change from that of consultant to advocate if the student's performance is failing. As we work towards a system which expects that all students' practice will be supervised by accredited practice teachers, questions are being raised about the need for tutors to be subject to a system of accreditation (see Montgomery and Rea, 1992).

Occasionally, due to leave commitments or sickness, the practice teacher is unavailable for supervision. This situation can be discussed at the pre-placement stage and a substitute nominated who can then be familiarised with the pattern of supervision and its recording. Similarly, the student may undertake a specialist project or piece of work which is better supervised by the appropriate practitioner or specialist; arrangements can be made to incorporate such colleagues' feedback on student performance, verbally or in written form. It is of course important to clarify roles and responsibilities in advance of such arrangements. Equally the practice teacher as overall manager of the students' learning experience needs to be able to decide how and when to use the information provided by colleagues.

Techniques and Tools

It is likely that the most common form of supervision is the one-to-one model of discussion between practice teacher and student, based on verbal presentation which is case or work-focused and includes the prospective (what might be done) and the retrospective (what was done). Specialist or semi-specialist practice teachers may have the opportunity, while working with more than one student at a time, to make use of joint (two students) or group supervision. Similarly, individual practice teachers can come together in pairs or groups with their students. This can enable the development of a constructively critical environment where peers contribute directly to each other's learning and development, and hold a responsibility for being critical of one another.

If such a situation works well (and it needs working at), it can empower students and enable a degree of learning which would not be possible in the one-to-one situation. Good practice suggests, however, that to work well it requires forward planning and a clarity of roles and responsibilities. Student Units have typically used this approach and it can also be seen in some educational settings. The enquiry and action learning approach uses a problem-based learning which:

> *aims to integrate more effectively college work and practice learning, to build on the knowledge and skills students bring to the course and to help them become self-directed lifelong learners, able to adapt to the changing demands that will be placed on them as professionals.*
> (Burgess and Jackson, 1990: p3)

Whether in the one-to-one or on a joint/group basis, supervision often revolves around the student's need for information, guidance and feedback. This is particularly so in the early stages of training, or when the student is new to the agency. It is likely that the most common form of supervision is the one-to-one model of discussion between practice teacher and student, based on verbal presentation which is case or work-focused. It is important, however, to be aware that, as the placement progresses, the supervision sessions should be moving on, for example, to explore issues and themes, concentrating on one or two topics of social work practice, or spent in direct teaching of social work method, statutory and legal elements of the work, the theory of organisations or institutions, and so on. As supervision progresses, the student should be initiating the direction of his/her learning and playing a greater part in sharing or suggesting supervision agendas.

It is important for practice teachers to make use of all available resources and tools for supervision. The social work profession in general has been poor at sharing its experience and learning from practice, often 'reinventing the wheel' – although this is improving. Within practice teaching, there is a body of resources available through Practice

Curriculum developments, and these provide a range of very good material applicable to all social work settings (see Doel and Shardlow, 1993 and Hall et al, 1991). Indeed an exercise or simulation is not difficult to put together yourself if it is kept simple; practice teachers have often evolved their own materials and it can be helpful to share these through practice teacher support groups or resource exchanges.

Be aware also of checklists, structures, exercises that are available within your own agency for colleague use. Within the probation service, for example, training packs containing useful handouts, overhead projector slides and exercises have been made available on a national basis with the introduction of both the Criminal Justice Act 1991 and its subsequent amendments. Similarly, some probation teams have adopted a thematic approach to supervision so that, over a given period, all cases or work considered in supervision will focus on a particular aspect of work, for example, anti-discriminatory practice or throughcare with prisoners, and can then be the focus of individual and team supervision.

While the student's presentation of his/her work is very often in written form, this can vary from agency recording, to a process record, to the practice teacher's specific request for a write-up on a particular aspect of work with the client, family or group. The presentation can also be done through audio or video recording and such methods are increasingly requested as direct evidence of student work. Joint work with a colleague, whether as a consultant or a co-worker, can usefully be evaluated with the colleague present at the supervision session. Various methods of evaluation will be considered in greater detail in the next chapter.

The presentation of work and its discussion can be achieved in a number of creative ways. A flipchart or board can be a useful tool to enable the practice teacher or student to describe, for example, a family history by using the family tree, eco maps to place individuals in their system, or any personalised chart of a group or individual session. Sculpting, using the practice teacher, student, and colleagues if necessary, is another way of enabling the student's learning (see Chapter 6).

Beware of having only discussion in supervision. Adults learn in a range of different ways and variety in presentation can enable the student to think about a problem in a completely different and often creative way, thereby unblocking thought processes and leading to different ways of working. When we have a student who just does not seem to grasp what we are saying, we tend to do 'more of the same' and simply explain it in a different way. If this is still not helpful, do something different – draw what you are explaining, act it out or sculpt it! Be imaginative; supervision can be good fun as well as hard work.

Checklist

It may be useful to review supervision periodically by addressing the following questions. These are designed to be answered by the practice teacher but you may find it useful to design a similar checklist for student use.

Content

- Is supervision regular as planned? Does it keep to time and is it uninterrupted?
- Is the level of informal supervision appropriate?
- Are colleagues providing feedback; do they need to be involved in the supervision session?
- Am I, and is the student, preparing for supervision and undertaking the interim tasks?
- Are there other resources I can use – for example, exercises, simulations, training materials?
- Are agendas and records of supervision being prepared and maintained?
- If not, what is preventing this and how can it be changed?

Process

- Am I able to identify movement in the student; are supervision sessions progressing or maintaining the same focus?
- What sort of learner is the student and how does this fit with my style?
- Is the student able to conceptualise ideas and transfer learning to other areas of practice?
- What is the student's attitude towards, and contribution to, supervision?
- What areas of learning need to be introduced or further developed?

Chapter 6

Methods of Evaluation

This is the first of two chapters devoted to the rather thorny issue of evaluation or assessment of the student's performance. Chapter 7 will examine the structure, content and rationale of evaluation – the when, what and why. This chapter sets the scene for that discussion by exploring the 'how' of evaluation, the range of possible methods, old and not so old, for achieving a fair and accurate picture of the student's strengths and weaknesses, that is, the capabilities to be nurtured and the areas in need of development.

The rules and requirements for the Diploma in Social Work, as set out in Paper 30, stress that:

> *To qualify for the award of the DipSW, students must demonstrate that they have the competence to practise as social workers.*
>
> (CCETSW, 1991: p25)

Indeed, CCETSW now require that a students practice is:

> *directly and systematically observed by a practice teacher ... In residential, day care and community settings it has always been the case that students' practice has been visible. Views about confidentiality have often inhibited this practice from being extended to other settings, particularly where they involve one-to-one work with individual clients or delicate work with families. CCETSW now requires that this practice is extended to all settings. However, it requires that the dignity and confidentiality of clients must be safeguarded.* (p26)

There are a number of means by which students can demonstrate their competence and enable the practice teacher to evaluate their abilities.

Written Records

Written records can take a number of forms but the main ones are:

a) case records

b) reports (social histories, pre-sentence reports, and so on)

c) letters

d) process recordings

In placements where case records are not used, it is likely there will be other forms of accounts of work done. Where it is not the normal practice of agencies to request such accounts of work done, the practice teacher can of course specifically request such records for teaching and assessment purposes.

Records can be a good indication of how well a student has grasped a particular social work situation, how much planning has been geared towards it and how appropriate these plans seem to be. However, a strong word of caution is required here. It would be a grave error to judge a student's work primarily on the basis of written records as they can be very misleading. A good practitioner may lack the writing skills to do justice in writing to his/her work or a poor practitioner may be able to 'dress up' his/her records and thereby conceal poor practice. It has been known for students to present excellent accounts of interviews which never actually took place. It is therefore vital to use records as only one part of an overall scheme of assessment involving a number of elements rather than the mainstay. As we shall stress in the next chapter, evaluation of a student's performance must be based on evidence and the wider the range and scope of evidence, the better. An over-reliance on written records is therefore to be avoided.

Moreover, written records should be an indirect basis of assessment, as it should be the discussions in supervision relating to these records which give strong clues about the student's strengths and weaknesses in particular areas. The student will have the opportunity to elaborate on the records and discuss the issues they raise. Written records are therefore a primary focus for both teaching and assessment.

Before moving on from written records, it is worth devoting some attention to the issue of using process recordings. Such records are often seen as being old-fashioned, especially in this 'hi-tech' era. However, we suspect that the decline in their use owes more to misuse than to fashion or technology. They are often seen as being time-consuming and of little use but much of this disfavour seems to stem from the confusion between a process record – which can be very valuable – and a verbatim record – which is of very limited value.

The aim of a process recording is to provide a record of the process of an interview which should then illustrate the dynamics of the interview and the thoughts and feelings which lie behind these dynamics. A verbatim record is therefore unnecessary and wasteful. The student should seek to:

- remember (and record immediately after the interview) what happens in the interview in terms of:

- the initial strategy of the interview (purpose, style and focus)

- the process of development it follows (the 'logic' of the interview, the emotional responses, the body language, and so on.)

- the conclusion (style and timing of ending, focus for future work, and so on)

Students need to be encouraged (and perhaps taught) to record the dynamic process of the interview rather than a blow by blow account of the 'she said so I said' variety.

A successful process recording can provide excellent insights into:

- the assumptions the student makes
- the style of reasoning he/she adopts
- his/her handling of emotions
- the student's communication skills
- his/her ability to control an interview in a focused way
- the student's level of confidence (and degree of comfort in the social work role).

The potential value of these insights for both teaching and evaluation makes process recording, if handled properly, an excellent tool for the practice teacher.

Direct Observation and Live Supervision

One of the frequent criticisms of using written records as a basis of evaluation is that there is a possibility (or even probability) that such recordings are not an accurate account as they may be biased, whether deliberately or otherwise. They are, after all, a subjective account.

A more objective report of the work done can obviously be gained if the practice teacher is present and actually witnesses the student in action. It is important, however, to distinguish between direct observation of the student by the practice teacher or colleague, and the role of live supervision. The former should ensure that the practice teacher does not intervene but sits back from the interview or student input, remaining silent. Any exception to this should be negotiated in advance, for example, where any element of risk (to student or client) is introduced during the interview.

With live supervision, the agreement between the student and practice teacher is quite different. The session is designed primarily to enhance the student's learning 'there and then', and enable, for example, a change of direction, or the introduction of a different approach. With direct observation, such learning can only take place retrospectively. In live supervision, it is therefore vital for both the student and practice teacher to be clear who is to do what and why. The student may, for example, be the lead worker, with the practice teacher only intervening on a strategic basis. Both workers need to be clear whether the practice teacher is making a suggestion or issuing an instruction, and they need to have agreed how any intervention will be signalled by the practice teacher. Careful explanation should ensure that, during the interview, the client(s) should be aware of, and understand, the approach being used, so that the student can remain in control of the session. Any questions or comments from the client(s) to the practice teacher should be redirected to the student.

Whether live supervision or direct observation, the period after the interview or input is as important to the student's learning as the pre-interview preparation. This provides opportunities not only for feedback, but also self-evaluation. Learning can be identified and additional learning needs acknowledged. Future planning for work with the client(s) can take place close to direct experience of them, rather than hours or days later in the supervision session.

A common objection to direct observation or live supervision is that the student is 'under the microscope' and this may have an adverse effect on his/her performance. However, we should remember that dealing with anxiety-provoking situations is a skill all social workers need to develop; therefore this should not be a major barrier provided that the practice teacher is prepared to make allowances for 'nerves' where appropriate.

Another concern is that the situation may seem artificial to the client(s) and this in turn may affect the way the student handles the situation. This only underlines the importance of the student's careful advance preparation with the client(s), which should include obtaining their consent. Experience suggests that we are far more worried than our clients about such a situation, and the client will often readily take part in the experience, perhaps recognising that they can give something back to the student by contributing to their learning.

Joint Work

One of the benefits of direct observation and live supervision is that they can involve a practice teacher's colleagues, particularly relevant where the student is working at a distance from the practice teacher, or is involved with a colleague in a specialist piece of work or project. It is always important in such circumstances to be clear about the role and responsibilities of the practice teacher's colleague, who can provide the student with learning from an area of expertise not held by the practice teacher. For the practice teacher, it can also provide an alternative perspective on the student's abilities and can be a safeguard against subjectivity on the part of the practice teacher.

The practice teacher or colleague might also undertake joint work with the student where each takes responsibility for different aspects of a case or piece of work. Such an approach can be particularly useful at first placement stage, or when the student's abilities with a client group or setting are untested. The student might, for example, contribute to a piece of work or case by undertaking concrete, practical tasks in the first instance. It is important, however, to build on his/her learning by enabling the degree or extent of their involvement to develop whenever appropriate. In this way, different skills can be tested and learning developed – often as a useful precursor to live supervision with the same client(s).

Audio and Video Recording

The same issue of anxiety or 'stage-fright' reappears here but so also does the retort that students need to learn to cope with anxiety.

The disadvantage of artificiality can also be voiced, but practitioners and trainers who make frequent use of audio and video equipment tend to find that the microphone and camera soon seem to fade into the background and the participants often comment that they soon forgot they were being taped. Nonetheless, it may be necessary for the student, and ideally the client(s), to become familiar and at ease with the setting, and perhaps the equipment, in order to facilitate this 'fading into the background'.

The advantages of audio and video recording are that a clear record, unaffected by subjective bias, is presented and of course can be re-presented. Live supervision cannot be repeated – there is no 'action replay' to aid discussion; whereas audio and video recordings can be paused or rewound and replayed in order to clear up any doubts or clarify any confusions.

The big disadvantage, of course, is that these methods can be extremely time-consuming. For example, analysing and discussing a thirty minute interview may take up to two and a half hours. Consequently there are clear restrictions on taking full advantage of audio and video equipment as tools for teaching and evaluation. It is possible, however, to focus, for example, on the beginning, mid-point or ending of an interview or input, or to agree to concentrate on a theme within a session which illustrates a particular aspect of the student's learning.

Video recording is more useful than audio insofar as the former includes very important visual clues – that is, audio recording omits the important dimension of body language. However the strength of audio recording lies in its relative cheapness, easier accessibility and mobility. Many also find it less intrusive than video recording.

These ways of recording work are not ideal but they can act as a useful and effective means of complementing the other methods of ensuring that the practice teacher is in touch with the student's practice.

Self-assessment

It should be understood that the practice teacher's final written report evaluating the student's practice will reach its own (supported) conclusions concerning the student's ability to reach the required standard. The student is also expected to draw evidence from his/her own practice in order to demonstrate competence. Self-assessment is therefore an important component and should form a regular part of supervision as well as the formal reports prepared for the Assessment Board. Feedback to the student should be an integral part of his/her practical experience and should never come as a pleasant or unpleasant surprise on reading the practice teacher's final report. Should there be a disparity between the practice teacher's assessment of the student and his/her own, this should be clearly documented during the placement in supervision notes, and should also feature as part of placement meetings with the tutor.

Client/Consumer Assessment

In principle, a client/consumer assessment of the student's competence can be a valuable part of any evaluation of student performance. In reality, it is difficult to achieve for a number of reasons. Which clients/consumers should be involved – the one or two willing to be involved, a representative sample, all of them? Who is the client or consumer – should it, for example, include case conference members or the sentencers who receive the student's reports? Would some client groups be impossible to include – because of the nature of their involvement with the agency, or the identified problem? While the practice teacher is evaluating competence as defined by CCETSW's rules and requirements, clients may well apply different criteria – whether the student is nice, whether he/she 'got them off' at court, whether he/she left them alone or visited everyday. The student might meet the client's criteria but, in so doing, have not achieved what was expected or required of them in role.

This is not to say that client/consumer assessment has no place, but that it is one of the most difficult aspects of evaluation. It is possible for clients to have their say and make measured and useful assessments, and for the consumer in the wider sense (case conference members or sentencers, for example) to make a valid contribution. As with all aspects of evaluation so far considered, the key is in the planning, preparation and clarity of purpose undertaken by the practice teacher and student. As a practice teacher, it is also important to think creatively about the potential for such contributions within your own setting.

Creative Methods

Although the methods we have indicated above are by far the most common and popular, they are by no means the only ones. Some practice teachers adopt a very imaginative approach and then 'the sky's the limit'. We shall restrict ourselves here to a brief discussion of two such methods as examples of less conventional approaches.

As mentioned in the previous chapter, the technique of 'sculpting' used in family therapy can be used not only as a therapeutic strategy with clients but also as a means of recounting or reconstructing, within a supervision session, a situation encountered in practice. Objects (or, if there are enough willing volunteers available, colleagues) can be used to represent members of a family or group and can be arranged to represent in graphic form the relative position of the family members and the movements relative to each other which occur during the process of the interview. The dynamics of the family situation and of the interview are re-enacted in a mini-drama. The student's perception of the situation and his/her strategy and style of intervention soon become apparent when this method of supervision/evaluation is used. (For a fuller account of sculpting, see Walrond-Skinner, 1976).

Drawing can also be used, in much the same way, to represent the dynamics of a situation and how these change in response to the student's intervention. This is particularly effective for students who, perhaps in their early days of a placement, find it difficult to verbalise about the complex situations they encounter in practice. It is a form of communication which can produce very good results, can be conducted in a 'fun' atmosphere and can pave the way for more conventional and sophisticated modes of communication. There is of course a very clear parallel here with techniques used in direct work with children and cartooning with offenders.

What by now should be very clear is that practice teachers have available to them a wide repertoire of methods which can be called upon to form as reliable and accurate a picture as possible of the student's strengths and weaknesses. The main danger to be avoided has already been mentioned and that is the risk of a too narrow reliance on one of these methods without reference to the others. It is of course not necessary to use all the methods, but the course examiners will need evidence to support whatever decision is made about the student's progress – be it pass or fail – and so it behoves the practice teacher to ensure that sufficient steps have been taken to gain an adequate assessment. These measures are available to facilitate such steps.

Of course, the variety of methods is consistent with our earlier discussions of learning styles and the variety of ways in which adults learn. Creative methods may not suit everyone, but they may be very useful for working with those who do not find traditional methods very helpful.

Chapter 7

Evaluation of Student Performance

On a quiet afternoon in a probation office, a client had failed to turn up for an appointment. The practice teacher and his student, who had some slight social contact prior to the placement, were filling the gap in their day with some idle conversation. At one point, the practice teacher sighed and said: "You know, I like you a lot; I'm going to hate giving you a bad report".

The student (who happens to be one of the present authors) learned much from the subsequent discussion of shortcomings in performance – but also had a vivid illustration of the need for (and, in this case, the ability of) a practice teacher to keep his/her mind firmly on the task of assessment, regardless of personal feelings. For there is little doubt that one of the difficulties which occurs in supervision is that practice teachers and students, working closely together for weeks or months on end, frequently form close and friendly relationships – yet, in the last analysis, an objective assessment of professional performance and capacity is sought at the end of the placement.

It will help the process of assessment if four considerations are borne in mind at the outset:

First, the relationship is a professional one. This need not preclude (indeed, it may be helped by) feelings of mutual liking or respect, joint participation in the office card-school or badminton team or whatever. It must, of course, also be able to survive and not be prejudiced by differences of personality or viewpoint. However, just as the social worker may maintain warm relationships with his/her clients yet still preserve the element of professional detachment necessary to make an informed judgement, so must the practice teacher remember that he/she is engaged in a professional task, and one carrying considerable responsibilities.

Second, these responsibilities must be remembered. As so often in social work, they are multiple: responsibility to agency, to course, to student – but above all else to clients, present and future. In our view, this last is paramount: the practice teacher may be managing a learning experience for the student's immediate benefit, but this is part of a process aimed at producing a competent social worker. If the student has not yet reached an adequate level of competency, the practice teacher must not be afraid to say so. The benefit of any doubt cannot be given to the student, however strong the temptation, born of sympathy, to do so may be; it belongs to the student's future clients.

Third, however, is the fact that the practice teacher is not (or should not be) working in isolation. The next chapter notes the sources of support available, and emphasises the desirability of sharing responsibility.

Fourthly, to this may be added one more thought: the practice teacher is only called upon to comment on student performance – not on his/her private life, morals, personality or beliefs (unless they impinge on that performance). A former golfer was once quoted as saying: "A man may miss a three-foot putt on the last hole of a Ryder Cup match, and still remain a good husband and father". To decide that someone is not performing well as a social worker is not to say that he/she is one of the world's failures.

All these points may be more easily understood and applied if the practice teacher has a sound framework within which to set his/her assessment. It is tempting, and has frequently been the practice in the past, to use some fairly subjective criteria: would I want him in my team? would I want her as my social worker? While, in reality, this type of reference point will continue to exist in people's minds, there has been an increasing movement towards analysis of the skills and level of achievement necessary to satisfy the requirements of a beginning worker.

The Statement of Requirements for Qualification in Social Work (CCETSW Paper 30) defines the competence required by newly qualified social workers in all settings and sectors. To achieve their Diploma in Social Work qualification, trainee social workers will be expected to acquire and demonstrate:

- core knowledge, values and skills;

- competence in assessing, planning, intervening and evaluating outcomes;

- competence in working with individuals, families and groups over a substantial period in an area of particular practice within the relevant legal and organisational frameworks and

- competence in transferring knowledge and skills to new structures and in taking responsibility for their professional practice.

(CCETSW, 1991: p9).

Whilst Paper 30 sets out CCETSW's expectations of colleges and agencies as programme providers, it does not prescribe a particular model of training. Rather, it focuses on the process and content of assessment in the hope of encouraging a flexible approach to the provision of programmes:

"The requirements are designed to encourage a range of innovative approaches within the context of joint college/agency partnerships and common assessment requirements." (p10)

Each programme has to outline how students will be assessed in relation to the requirements. There are two formal assessment points in any programme: intermediate and final assessments. Unless there are exceptional circumstances, a student cannot embark on the final piece of assessed practice without succeeding at the intermediate stage. The main purpose of the intermediate assessment is to identify any student who has not achieved an agreed pass standard by that stage in the programme and, in so doing, evaluate the progress being made towards achieving the objectives of the programme. While programme providers can choose a range of assessment methods for the intermediate stage, they have to include:

- a written report by the practice teacher evaluating the student's practice, and

- written work demonstrating the student's understanding of relevant knowledge and theory as applied to social work practice.

At the point of final assessment, the programme's Assessment Board will determine whether the student has reached a satisfactory level in each of the areas defined in the Statement of Requirements through consideration of:

- a substantial piece of written work, drawn from the student's area of particular practice, demonstrating the student's capacity to relate theory and practice;

- other written work required in accordance with the programme's assessment regulations;

- evidence from practice provided by the student, and

- a report from the practice teacher during the period of assessed practice and indicating clearly whether or not the student has reached the required standard. The report must be based on selected aspects of the student's practice which have been directly observed by the practice teacher and which relate to the elements in the Statement of Requirements. Direct observation of the student's practice by another practice teacher must be used as supporting evidence where a student's performance is marginal or below the pass standard.

(from Para 3.4.3.2).

Every programme uses a model of assessment based on the Statement of Requirements – knowledge, values, core skills, and competence in social work practice. But courses will differ in terms of the structure and style of their assessment model. Within a common framework, practice teachers will notice differences of emphasis and detail, and a variety of means of grading the student's ability. For example, some programmes differentiate the student's performance on two levels: has, or has not yet, achieved competence (pass or fail); others draw on three levels: very weak (unacceptable), satisfactory (pass) and strong (outstanding). Some even go so far as to use four levels: not competent, not yet competent, competent (beginning) and competent (experienced). In attempting to live up to CCETSW's expectation that a rigorous assessment of practice is critical to maintaining the credibility of the qualifying award, each assessment system makes use of supporting structures. Many then dictate the format of the placement report, for example, through the use of a tick-sheet approach to listed competences, or by guiding the practice teacher with suggested positive and negative indicators of competence.

By way of illustration, we shall present a modified version of the model previously developed by the present authors in the first edition of this book. However, it should be remembered that this is an illustration of only one approach amongst many. Each course will have its own *schema* and practice teachers will need to familiarise themselves with the details of the framework of the particular programme they are working with.

Within our framework (as detailed in Appendix 3), the practice teacher is asked to assess the student's performance in nine aspects of practice which are seen as central to satisfactory functioning within the profession.

Professional Values and Attitudes are central to social work practice; the Statement of Requirements states that:

> *Competence in social work requires the understanding and integration of the values of social work. This set of values can essentially be expressed as a commitment to social justice and social welfare, to enhancing the quality of life of individuals, families and groups within communities, and to a repudiation of all forms of negative discrimination.*

(CCETSW, 1991: p15)

Gender stereotyping, racism, bigotry, refusal to see another's viewpoint and so on, will impair the ability to operate in the ways expected of a competent social worker. In particular, such attitudes will stand in the way of the development of anti-discriminatory practice, and will therefore act as a barrier to acceptable professional practice. Indeed, anti-discriminatory and anti-oppressive values are a central theme of this aspect of practice assessment.

Instrumental skills in *Communication, Assessment and Intervention* are obviously necessary attributes of the practitioner. Such skills, however, need to be seen and assessed in the context of, for example, ethnically sensitive practice and indeed other aspects of anti-discriminatory practice.

Self-Management Skills and Ability to Work within the Agency are also needed if the student is to be able to function effectively as a colleague and as a worker. Using resources, both personal and institutional, to best effect is increasingly becoming an important part of the social worker's skill repertoire.

Use of Supervision is an essential part of the learning process and provides an excellent opportunity for addressing learning needs, identifying areas of competence and establishing a strong base line of anti-discriminatory practice.

The Ability to Relate Theory and Practice is a central part of developing professional competence by being able to draw on relevant theoretical frameworks and research, and developing critical thinking skills. This is also important in terms of ensuring that a theoretical understanding of disadvantage, inequality and oppression is translated into anti-discriminatory practice.

Development as a Social Worker is self-evidently important in the context of a placement and of student identity – but, since the capacity for professional learning and personal growth are held to be necessary attributes of all practitioners, it is also an essential attribute of the future worker. Also, as was noted in Chapter 2, the ability to 'unlearn', to break free from previous socialisation and stereotypes, is a key aspect of developing an anti-discriminatory approach to practice.

Some approaches to assessment include a specific section on anti-discriminatory and anti-oppressive practice to ensure that such issues are directly and explicitly addressed. The model we present here operates on the basis of a 'permeation' strategy: that is, such issues are incorporated into all aspects of assessment in an attempt to ensure integration and avoid tokenism. Each approach has relative strengths and weaknesses, but the important point to note for present purposes is that, whatever *schema* you are using, it is essential that issues of anti-discriminatory practice are incorporated. Both good practice and CCETSW requirements make this both necessary and desirable.

So far, then, we have an analysis of the components of professional practice. But how do we tackle the more difficult and fundamental problems of deciding what is 'satisfactory'? This model, like others, offers illustrative guidelines – positive and negative indicators to help the practice teacher arrive at what must, ultimately, be his/her professional decision. Since expectations of first and final placement students will obviously differ, different sets of indicators are provided for each.

Let us take, briefly and partially, the relatively straightforward question of communication skills as an example of the system at work. Positive indicators for satisfactory performance in a first-year student include the ability to listen, an understanding (perhaps at this stage intuitive rather than thought out) of non-verbal communication, the ability to convey factual information clearly to clients, to state information and arguments in discussion, and to write clear, straightforward reports. Evidence for this might come from watching a student in a joint interview and learning afterwards what cues had been picked up, or from discovering that a client clearly understood information that the student had passed on, or from finding his/her reports intelligible, easy to follow, and to the point.

Negative indicators for the first placement include lack of awareness of clients' verbal and non-verbal messages, over-hesitancy or 'talking through people' when speaking to clients, inadequate or confusing reports. Again evidence may come from similar sources: that the student is not showing a satisfactory level of communication skills who has not understood, or who has not 'heard' what the client is trying to say, or who talks jargon to a bewildered client, or who has to be constantly asked to explain or supplement verbally his/her written reports.

Reference to Appendix 4 will show the application of similar indicators to other areas of practice. Essentially, the guidelines provide some link between the concept of the desired skill – communication or whatever – and the day-to-day work of the student and practice teacher. By showing how good or bad performance may manifest itself, they make it easier to identify examples to support assessment (and the importance of evidence, while mentioned elsewhere, may be reiterated here). Thus it becomes easier for the practice teacher to say:

"Paula has good written communication skills: her reports were always concise, lucid and accurate; but her verbal communication needs improvement: twice I had to explain to clients simple information she had passed on but they had not understood and, when arguing her case in a team meeting, she became diffident, confusing and ultimately ineffective".

Now, Paula's case may not be uncommon: a good-in-places, curate's egg of a performance. The indicators help sort out what is good and what is bad; they will identify the outstanding student who clearly passes, and the very poor performer who must fail. The vast majority will fall somewhere in between – and there is no escaping the need to exercise professional judgement. Is the level of performance satisfactory, *in the view of the practice teacher and his/her supporting system,* for a student at this stage of training (that is, intermediate or final)? To stick with

Paula for a moment: assuming she is a first placement student, it may be that incidents of poor verbal communication were fairly isolated and that, in general, clients understood her. In that case, she can pass, with a note about her future learning needs. If, however, there are other examples, amounting to a general pattern of poor verbal communication, she is likely not to have reached the desired standard.

It must be emphasised, however, that assessment is not just an issue of passing or failing. Most students pass; all students still have something to learn. Therefore, the task of the practice teacher is more likely to involve identifying points of strength or weakness rather than hard decisions of failure (though this will occur: the issue is discussed in the next chapter). In the case of first placement students, guidance is in effect being given to the course and to future practice teachers as to what is still necessary, and this is widely understood and accepted. Rather less obvious is the importance in final placements of providing guidance for the newly-qualifying worker and his/her agency as to future development needs. The practice teacher who says, in effect, "Well done, you've passed; there's nothing to worry about", has not completed the task required, or given the student the service he/she needs or deserves.

The practice teacher's assessment plays an important role in determining the student's future. The practice teacher's recommendations are to:

"Stand in their own right as recommendations to the programme assessment board' (CCETSW, 1991: p26)

If the practice teacher considers the student's practice to be marginal or likely to fail, the Requirements state that a second opinion should be sought from another practice teacher. In some cases, this second opinion is provided from within the practice teacher's own agency or organisation; in others, it is made available externally. The Assessment Board does have the power to go against a practice teacher's recommendation in the sense that the board's role is to examine the student's progress overall, taking account of all the information available to them. Where a student's performance is seen by the practice teacher as below standard or marginal, he/she should be invited to attend the Assessment Board meeting to contribute to the discussion.

To sum up this chapter: in taking on the role of practice teacher, the worker accepts responsibility for assessing a student's performance. It is a professional task, requiring the exercise of professional judgement. Like other professional tasks, it is likely to be best performed within a clear and well understood frame of reference, and if suitable support systems are available and utilised. Like other social work assessments, this must be based upon the best available evidence, and that evidence needs to be relevant to the assessment and as objectively based as possible. Occasionally the assessment process will require hard decisions and may produce unhappiness (though no more so than other situations in, say, child care or probation). More usually, it will provide an opportunity to help the career development of a fellow member of the social work profession.

Chapter 8

Troubleshooting: Dealing with Difficulties

Most placements are relatively trouble-free and unproblematic but of course there are always the exceptions, the minority of placements which throw up difficulties, complications and worries. Probably the greatest anxiety of practice teachers hinges on the question of: 'What do I do when problems arise?'. The main difficulty practice teachers seem to fear is that of the student whose performance is unsatisfactory and the issue of failure arises. This is a situation we need to address, as it can place great strain on all concerned.

However, it would be a mistake to assume that the issue of 'the failing student' is by any means the only one that can arise. The practice teacher faces a number of potential problems and therefore it is important to be prepared and equipped for the type and range of problems which crop up from time to time. The aim of this chapter is to take some steps towards helping practice teachers get to grips with some of the more common but very thorny problems that can be encountered, although obviously we cannot cover all eventualities.

We shall first of all discuss the support systems upon which practice teachers should be able to draw and the strategies which can be adopted to minimise the risk of problems arising, or at least to 'nip them in the bud'. We shall then move on to look at each of the most likely problems to arise, how these tend to manifest themselves and how they can be tackled. This will pave the way for our conclusion, which will bring together the strands of our discussion of dealing with the difficulties placements sometimes generate.

In theory at least, the practice teacher has access to a number of support systems:

1. Colleagues
2. Line manager(s)
3. The tutor
4. Other practice teachers

How well developed and effective these networks are will vary a great deal depending on the setting and on the practice teacher's own willingness to make use of them where they exist and to press for them where they do not.

The practice teacher has responsibility for the placement, but this is not a sole responsibility. The student is placed within a particular team, establishment or agency and, as with any other piece of work undertaken, colleagues should be willing and able to support the practice teacher with advice, feedback, discussion and, where needed, practical and moral or emotional support. It is as well for the practice teacher to know where he/she stands before agreeing to act as practice teacher.

Similarly one's line manager in particular and managers in general have a duty to provide support especially at times when difficulties are being experienced. Practice teaching should not be an exception to this, as one is acting on behalf of the agency in much the same way as one would with any aspect of the workload. It may be necessary, however, to sensitise one's line manager to these issues and perhaps gain his/her commitment before agreeing to a placement request. The advice, experience and agency authority of a line manager may be particularly helpful when a problem scenario presents itself.

The support of the student's personal tutor should be readily available (but see below for more about this) both at the pre-defined times, such as a mid-placement review, and at any other reasonable time when difficulties arise. In fact, it is wise to keep the tutor informed of such problems or potential problems even if you are not intending to draw him/her into the fray at that stage. Informing the student of this contact with the tutor may serve to bring it fully to the student's attention that steps need to be taken to rectify the situation or prevent it from deteriorating further, although hopefully the practice teacher will have discussed these issues openly with the student before involving the tutor.

A great deal of assistance can also be gained from discussion with other practice teachers who may be experiencing or may have experienced similar or related problems. Even where no similar experience of such problems can be found, the opinions or advice of peers can help gain a fresh or wider perspective on the situation. The feelings of solidarity and comfort such consultations with other practice teachers can produce are not to be underestimated. Where a number of practice teachers operate in close proximity, for example within the same office, district or town, support groups may be set up to share ideas, ventilate anxieties and generally learn from each other. The development of accreditation procedures and the supervision of practice teachers has led to quite a significant increase in the incidence of such groups as the whole enterprise of practice teaching is being more closely monitored and supported.

There are therefore, in theory at least, a number of support systems which can be called upon if necessary. The main barrier which can prevent a practice teacher from connecting with these systems is his/her own reluctance. There are perhaps a number of reasons for this, but whatever these may be, there is no shortage of examples of practice teachers who do not seek the help available.

Having reviewed the possibilities of obtaining support when problems are encountered, let us take a look at some of the strategies which can be used in a proactive way to deal with problems before they cause harm or become unmanageable.

The first step towards a satisfactory placement is, of course, the contract. Here the problems which may be presented by, for example, a weak or even a complacent student can be identified and a strategy developed jointly by student, tutor and practice teacher. These can be incorporated in the contract itself – forewarned is forearmed. Where problems are anticipated, the contract should reflect this, so that there will be no doubt or confusion as the placement progresses.

A second important strategy is to ensure that all communication is open and shared. Where three people are involved (practice teacher, student and tutor) there is always a risk of collusion, of two parties taking sides against the third (see Ward, 1979) and, where this does occur, problems can be made much worse as the strong feelings aroused can lead to recriminations and counter-recriminations. None of this is conducive to effective learning. Clear channels of communication with no secrets or hidden agendas are an important part of any placement but they can be crucial in dealing successfully with a problematic placement.

Third, it is important to keep records of supervision sessions – the issues raised, the discussions held and the conclusions drawn – to provide a firm basis of evidence of the way the placement has been handled to date. This will be of value to the tutor, or ultimately to the examiners, if called upon to respond to a dispute or difference of perspective between the student and practice teacher. Also, such records can provide useful background clues as to how the problem in question developed. Useful pointers or significant patterns which were not apparent at the time may be discernible on re-reading. Plotting the history of a problem can, of course, make a major contribution towards resolving it.

With experience, practice teachers should be able to develop a repertoire of such strategies and become quite adept at utilising them.

We now turn our attention to some problem areas which may need to be tackled as part of the practice teaching role. We have not attempted to produce a systematic typology of problems (which would be difficult due to the variations encountered). Rather, we have chosen to present this through a series of brief case examples. We believe these represent a fair cross-section of practice teaching experience – and the fact that they are identified, in several cases, by the rather informal shorthand titles we have adopted may serve to reinforce the reality that they are all founded in practical experience.

The failing student

Ray was an experienced worker when seconded to a professional course and, before his first placement, his tutor felt that he was having some difficulty in coping with his academic work. On placement, in a psychiatric setting, his experienced practice teacher became increasingly concerned about Ray's general level of practice and, in particular, his insistence that his present clients were 'different' because of their mental illness. Concern was first expressed by the practice teacher at a routine, three-party, tutorial visit; subsequently he asked for two more visits before the scheduled final assessment. The tutor was able to observe and participate in what was in effect a supervision session; he saw the problems for himself and agreed with the practice teacher that the student was unable to transfer learning from his previous setting to the new one. Discussions with the student alone confirmed his belief: Ray could not grasp that the family dynamics of mentally-ill people were akin to those of other clients. Like the practice teacher, the tutor concluded that Ray had learned to carry out certain functions effectively in his previous job, but was limited in his conceptual ability and carried rigid preconceptions about certain client groups. Practice teacher and tutor both spent a great deal of time trying, without much success, to explain to Ray why they felt his performance was unsatisfactory, but eventually both submitted recommendations to the Examining Board that he should fail. Although the Board offered another placement, Ray withdrew from the course in the face of simultaneous academic and practice failure, coupled with certain mainly personal problems.

This example illustrates very close co-operation between the practice teacher and the tutor, who was called in at an early stage and given every opportunity to see and understand the perceived problem, and time to put in additional work with the student in an attempt to overcome it. Each was able to draw conviction, in the final recommendation, from the knowledge that the other concurred in the decision. It also illustrates the existence of deep-rooted problems (intellectual limitation and rigidity of attitude) which are difficult and probably impossible to overcome: despite the Board's offer, it was unlikely that Ray could have succeeded on another placement; this was more than just a matter of correcting instrumental skills. Another not uncommon feature is the coincidence of prior academic concern, personal difficulties and poor practice performance. They may be difficult to disentangle, or it may be (as in this case) that they stem from common causes. The final point to be made is that both practice teacher and tutor felt that they had given all the help they could to Ray (the practice teacher the more so because he had certain experiences in common with his student) but, having done so without significant improvement in performance, they had no hesitation and no doubts in recommending that he fail.

The student who should fail

Joe was an amiable, slightly dreamy and impractical young man who was concerned, easy to get along with, but not very well-organised or decisive. After an uneventful but adequate course, he went to his final placement in a voluntary agency offering a community-based approach to its clients. He became a popular and accepted figure among the clients (staff felt he was often indistinguishable from them) but, although he made good relationships with them, he rarely translated these into the basis for action to ameliorate their conditions. Even in this informal setting, the practice teacher was worried about Joe's lack of professional presence and identity and his apparent reluctance to move into an active role. However, at tutorial visits, the tutor tended to be more interested in the agency's work and in Joe's perception of the clients than in focusing on performance. The practice teacher was uncertain in the face of this lack of tutorial lead; anyway, he liked Joe and thought he would not harm clients, and rationalised that Joe had not actually done anything 'wrong'. These views coloured his final report which, although equivocal in places, recommended a pass; despite some doubts expressed in the Board, there was felt to be no grounds for refusing to accept the practice teacher's recommendation. Subsequently, the practice teacher admitted doubts about his decision and that he felt that Joe needed longer to mature.

This is an example of sloppy practice on the part of practice teacher, tutor and, possibly, the Assessment Board. The practice teacher had failed to accept his responsibility for taking an active role in supervision or in assessing student performance (which must include both acceptance of professional identity and evidence of intervention skills), adopted a position based upon a benefit-of-the-doubt judgement of 'no actual reason to fail', and ultimately chose to avoid hurting the student's feelings and employment chances rather than facing the issue of his incompetence. The tutor was negligent, probably in allowing a placement which would enable Joe to avoid some of the issues he needed to confront (such as professional identity), certainly in allowing the placement to drift and in settling for a quiet life rather than taking a lead role in directing the course of the placement. Arguably, too, the Board accepted too readily the view that it needed very specific grounds for rejecting a practice teacher's recommendation, however ambiguous. Joe passed; he probably won't actively harm his clients – but he probably won't do them much good.

The duff tutor

Jill was a practice teacher of some experience, who agreed to take a student from a course which was new to her. The student was an older woman, with an interesting life history, little social work experience and a fairly high anxiety level. The information Jill received was skeletal, both about the course and about the student. A pre-placement visit was arranged which she anticipated would supplement the few facts available to her, but the tutor cried off because of another engagement and sent the student on her own. This was the student's first placement and Jill found that she was ill-prepared to discuss with the practice teacher her needs and aims of the placement. Jill was tempted to refuse the placement but felt sorry for the student and reluctant to punish her for the tutor's failing. Instead, she rang the course centre and demanded an instant visit. When the tutor arrived, she criticised his performance in very clear and logical terms and laid out her requirements in the way of information, joint planning and support. Embarrassed by his own culpability, and Jill's attack, the tutor was also surprised by her obvious commitment and professional competence as a practice teacher; attempting to redeem his reputation and salvage his pride, he responded by 'raising his own game' and working particularly conscientiously and efficiently. Not only did the student concerned benefit by a well-run placement, but the foundation was laid for a future relationship of mutual professional respect between Jill and the tutor.

This is an example of (perhaps too rare) initiative by the practice teacher to hold the tutor to account. Jill was prompt to recognise the early signs of inadequate tutor performance (poor initial preparation and neglect of pre-placement visit) and had the confidence in her own position and abilities to take him to task immediately. She knew what he should be doing and she insisted upon his doing it. She had two other options available – to refuse the placement completely, or to let it run with weak tutorial support. The one she chose was correct, in that it was the most constructive and most beneficial for the student. The outcome, in both short and long term, shows that professional relationships may be strengthened, rather than weakened, by an insistence on proper performance of assigned roles.

The sexist student

Hugh was a big, 'manly' man, with a good deal of experience before being seconded to his course. His sexism was not particularly crude or overtly offensive: it manifested itself in a gallant, sometimes protective or slightly patronising attitude to women on the course, characterised by mild flirtation and plenty of shoulder-hugging. His (female) tutor found this irritating, rather distrusted the respect he appeared to accord to her status, but chose to generally ignore or show mild contempt for his attitudes. On his first placement, Hugh was supervised by Alison – younger than he was and very competent in her own field. Sexism apart, she had decided that the age gap made it necessary for her to demonstrate clearly her own skills in social work, her confidence in the practice teacher role, and her dominant position in the professional relationship; her growing awareness of Hugh's chauvinism reinforced this view. Like the tutor, she avoided head-on challenge: she watched carefully for evidence of Hugh's attitudes carrying over into his work, but was satisfied that he could deliver a very effective and surprisingly unprejudiced service. Satisfied on this score, she decided that she would limit her attempts to modify his deep-seated attitudes to demonstrating a woman's ability to take a lead role and showing that she was not impressed by a 'macho' image. She felt that the time available on placement did not permit major attitude change, especially as she suspected (rightly) a failing marriage and foresaw the danger of being drawn into a counselling (or even sympathetic-understanding-woman) role.

The questions which may be debated here include the decisions, by both women, to ignore or take a low-key approach to Hugh's chauvinism: the tutor may have had less justification than Alison, since she had more time in which to work. However, it may also be argued that both were correct in saying that, since his sexist attitude to his peers and social acquaintances did not spill over into his practice, it was not disabling of him as a social worker. In this sense, the example of Hugh may represent a borderline case – but extreme, overt, cave-man examples of sexism will be less common than this socially-accepted jocular variety, since such individuals are more likely to be filtered out at selection. Decisions upon the point at which to challenge, how to challenge, whether to offer modification of attitudes by less confrontational means, such as demonstrations of competence in a non-traditional role, or possession of unprejudiced values by the practice teacher, have to be made in the light of prevailing circumstances – and by practice teachers of both sexes.

Collusion

Marion was a tutor of considerable experience who had had little contact with George, a mature student, before he was placed with Peter. Picking up contact unexpectedly when George's own tutor was ill, she felt at a disadvantage from the start with a placement she had not set up; she soon became worried that she was not learning enough about the work in hand. Both practice teacher and student were friendly and helpful, but she felt she could not pin them down: workload seemed light, reports seemed thin, she struggled to find the theoretical basis of their work. Yet when she put these and other points to them, there was always an answer, a reason, a reassurance that all was well. George particularly insisted that he was benefiting enormously from the placement, and some special needs he had specified were being met. Peter sometimes seemed puzzled and mildly hurt by her concern. She felt that she was being shut out – possibly because she was a woman and the two men were more comfortable together, possibly because George's past life had made him hypersensitive to possible criticism, possibly because they had something to hide, such as knowledge of a slack placement. She did not believe she was paranoid; she tried everything she could think of, from direct challenge about collusion to artful, circuitous questioning about George's cases. She complained to a colleague, 'I just don't know what is happening in that placement'. Even when later evidence from the next practice teacher suggested that Peter and George had done a satisfactory job, it still worried her that she never had a clear picture of what lay behind their wall.

Collusion can occur between any two of the three parties involved in a placement (or between all three, against a fourth party such as an Assessment Board, as may have been the case in an earlier example). It may occur for a number of reasons, such as shared distrust of the third party, or joint desire to conceal malpractice or idleness. There are real dangers of collusion between tutor and practice teacher if they have doubts about a student but lack the courage to bring them into the open; or between practice teacher and student if they have established a comfortable, undemanding relationship and fear the arrival of the tutor will put pressure on it; or between tutor and student if they lack confidence in the practice teacher and are reluctant to admit it openly. In most cases the party excluded will have some awareness of what is happening, will experience the frustrations felt by Marion, and may have similar difficulty in breaking down the barriers: collusion may require further collusion to deny it. This is a situation where prevention is far better than cure; clear, open channels of communication established at the outset, while they cannot guarantee that collusion will not occur, will be a great help in preventing it.

Personal problems

Jean's placement started well enough: she was energetic, exuberant, keen and good at the work, anxious to emphasise that her roles as wife and mother did not conflict with her capacity to do the job. The collapse was abrupt and tearful: after months of disharmony, carefully concealed from her professional contacts, her husband had left her; her children were distressed, her financial situation precarious and she needed to work through and adapt to her new situation. She told this to her practice teacher, Janet, 'in confidence', begged her not to let the course know, and asked for a few days to recover her balance before assuming the placement. Janet, with some reluctance, agreed – but it soon became apparent that Jean could not cope with the placement in her present state, that part of her anxiety related to failing the course as a consequence, and that she was attempting to use supervision sessions for personal counselling. Janet then insisted that the tutor be brought in, explaining the impossibility of her colluding with Jean against the course, and of fulfilling two roles. The tutor was quickly able to relieve Jean of some of her anxieties: the placement could be suspended, some other course work deferred, and arrangements made for Jean to resume her studies and her practice when she had resolved her domestic problems. Like Janet, he refused to accept a counselling role; but he was able to offer the option of the college counselling service as an alternative to the local marriage guidance service. Short of counselling, he and Janet were both able to offer support, sympathy and reassurance: there were plenty of precedents for students needing to take time out from their courses, and personal problems would not count against Jean or prevent her completing her training successfully when her life was on a more even keel.

Personal problems come in all forms: bereavement, unexpected pregnancy, illness, marital and other relationship problems, money troubles... Every case is different, but there are very few which cannot be sorted out satisfactorily. Almost invariably, the tutor and the course need to be involved: an interruption in the placement is an interruption of the course, and adjustments will need to be made to the student's overall learning experience. Moreover, the additional anxiety factor which troubled Jean ('How will this affect the course?') is so common a phenomenon as to be almost universal, and yet courses, from their long experience, can usually allay this swiftly. Jean's case illustrates another very common aspect: the attempt to draw practice teacher and tutor into

77

counselling roles. Both are likely to be vulnerable to such an approach, by nature of their own identity as 'helpers', and for this reason must be alert to the conflicts inherent in role duplication. The line between the helpful and supportive tutor and practice teacher on the one hand and the counsellor on the other is a fine one which must be carefully drawn.

Too good to be true

Marsha arrived on placement with glowing reports of her abilities, not only in the written information from her personal tutor, but also from the informal grapevine of personal contacts. She was a mature student with previous experience as a teacher, backed up with several years volunteer and probation assistant experience in a variety of settings; academically Marsha was said to be extremely bright. Within three weeks of the start of the placement Marsha seemed as if she had worked with her team for several years. She was popular with colleagues, and particularly with the general office staff. Her previous knowledge of the probation setting made her induction to the area very straightforward and she had, for example, already taken an active role in court duty while other students were content to concentrate on surviving the experience without embarrassing themselves or the agency they represented. The initial stages of her contacts with clients suggested that she had no problems in forming relationships, she was well aware of the legal and statutory basis of such relationships and was able to transmit her authority where necessary with clarity, concern and fair-mindedness. Marsha's overwhelming enthusiasm for the job naturally led her to suggest different ways of working with the office's clients and she had already volunteered to set up a group for the team's juvenile offenders. In supervision, Marsha's pace and enthusiasm for learning was always evident. Her practice teacher wondered what he could offer such a good student, particularly as her abilities and skills were far in advance of many of his colleagues, and she would obviously pass the placement even at this early stage.

Students of Marsha's ability are both a pleasure and a problem, in that they can inspire and motivate a practice teacher to assess his/her own practice and commitment to the job, extend his/her learning, and provide a 'boost' to a flagging team, but can also leave a practice teacher feeling overawed and ill at ease about his/her personal abilities as a practitioner and a teacher. The reaction can thus often be to step back and let the student 'get on with it'. A student coming to placement with a glowing reputation can also engender similar feelings in the tutor and, if care is not taken, an element of unspoken collusion between tutor and practice teacher could result in the student not being fully tested. If one partner, either tutor or practice teacher, is alone in their concerns about such a good student, it can make it almost impossible for them to challenge the student's performance.

Excellent students do exist but can still be given room to improve in their learning on placement: sometimes students have achieved reputations which bear close scrutiny. Reputations build up, often based on personal admiration or popularity, which then become part of a self-fulfilling prophecy – a halo effect. As caring professionals, we naturally look for the positives in our clients and our students and, when a student is good, we can have a predilection to overstress this factor and play down any negative aspects.

With the 'too good to be true' student, it is important for the practice teacher and tutor to:

a) examine closely where the initial assessment has been made and on what basis;

b) check that 'the basics' are given proper attention by the student, that is, do not assume understanding and abilities in, for example, assessment skills, record keeping, a clear social work value base;

c) be aware that some such students are very good at the immediately visible skills like beginning relationships, liaison with other agencies and teamwork, but have difficulty sustaining the day-to-day maintenance work with clients once the initial stages are passed;

d) work on the basis that any placement should encourage and look for movement in a student's learning. If the basics are sound, it is reasonable to push the good student and raise expectations of his/her practice, for example, encourage some developmental work on behalf of the team or agency (project work, community profile), ask the student to undertake specific reading for critical presentation in supervision, get him/her to address and debate the current social work issues. Identify with the student and the tutor how the boundaries of the good student's learning can be fully extended.

The duff agency

Martin was approached in the corridor one day by his senior and asked if he was interested in taking a student. His senior explained that a 'breakdown in communications' meant that the student needed to begin the placement the following week and that her situation was desperate. With misgivings Martin agreed to take the student who arrived for a meeting with her tutor on the day the placement began. Unfortunately due to a client crisis on the Friday before, Martin was unable to sort out a desk and chair for the student who had temporarily to take over the office of a colleague who was on leave. Martin approached his team colleagues about the student's arrival and felt supported by their words of encouragement. However, within a few days of the placement starting, the cases put forward by colleagues for the student were obviously those which nobody else wanted, that is, the most difficult clients to handle, with complex problems or those who were not keeping in contact. By the second week, because of pressures of work, Martin had missed two supervision sessions in a row with his student. He approached his senior to negotiate some workload relief but was told that his student would in time take work off him and, due to team commitments, no other relief would be possible.

A desire to help out and an interest in student training had led Martin to take on a commitment that could not be properly met. The 'breakdown in communications' turned out to be the fault of the agency which had promised a student placement and nominated a team without designating a named practice teacher. The senior had accepted the placement because she was keen to prove to her manager that her team could cope in any situation. Long before pre-placement stage, it is important to identify what the organisational responsibilities will be and what are the structural implications, negotiating with the proposed practice teacher on providing adequate practice facilities and resources, and in enabling the practice teacher to do a good job by recognising that students do not 'save' work but mean additional work for the practice teacher if the job is to be done properly.

Many agencies have established or are considering a system of workload relief for practice teachers, whether this is encompassed within the team or in the wider agency. Similarly it is necessary to involve a practice teacher's colleagues in negotiating a student's arrival. A stimulating and wide-ranging selection of workload for the student requires the commitment of all team members; greater emphasis on evaluation by co-workers, group workers, specialists or line consultants also needs the commitment and involvement of team colleagues. In Martin's case, he employed the help of the tutor to call a temporary stop to the placement in order to negotiate its future, first with his senior and then also with the team. The student had a three-week break which was made up by a slight extension to the placement. On her return, a proper contract of work, supervision and so on, was drawn up, which included the agency's formal responsibilities. Martin's senior also attended this contract meeting.

A racist experience

Yusuf had requested a busy, city placement with a varied workload and was pleased to be invited to a pre-placement meeting in just such a setting. It soon become obvious in discussion with the practice teacher that the all-white team would like Yusuf to undertake a special project for them, setting up and running an Asian resource centre on their patch. Yusuf began to wonder whose needs were being met by the placement and expressed the hope that he should also be given a wide range of client experience. The practice teacher assured him of this but, when pressed by the tutor, admitted that the project would need considerable input in its beginning stages. The team, however, were pleased to be getting a black student and had decided that, in order to combat the emphasis of a predominantly white agency, Yusuf should have his own black support network. A black worker from an allied agency had been asked to provide fortnightly contact with Yusuf and she would be included in supervision sessions every fourth week. The tutor was pleased that the practice teacher had taken into account the possible additional difficulties that a black student might face; Yusuf wondered whether he had any choice in the matter, as the black colleague was keen to help the team and to have links with the agency.

Four weeks into the placement, Yusuf's concerns were growing. The Asian Resource Project was taking up most of his time, particularly in providing networks, meeting community members and organising publicity, special meetings and so on. He had not had time to address the basic day-to-day tasks of the agency, although these were specified in his contract. The team were pleased with Yusuf's initial work on the project and he did not want to disappoint them by raising his objections. The black support worker meeting with Yusuf was helpful but seemed to have a different social work perspective to Yusuf's practice teacher and he was receiving contradictory messages. Yusuf was worried how these differences would be reconciled and whose evaluation of his practice would take precedence.

Eventually Yusuf raised these issues in supervision with his practice teacher and it was decided to include the tutor at a subsequent meeting. The practice teacher accepted that the project was taking up too much of Yusuf's time and also Yusuf's point that the team needed to be involved in the project in order to safeguard its continuance. However, Yusuf's concerns about the support worker were taken as an affront to the practice teacher's desire to combat institutionalised racism and she could not understand his objections. After lengthy discussion in which the tutor was able to present a slightly more distanced perspective, it was agreed that a measure designed to support a black student was, in practice, giving him 'two hoops to jump through' in the evaluation process. The practice teacher accepted that Yusuf should have been asked whether he wanted the support, what was available and how it would be used, rather than be faced with a *fait accompli*. The contract was renegotiated to decrease contact with the support worker and it specified that her role would concentrate on personal support rather than addressing practice issues. It was agreed that no evaluation was necessary from the support worker as part of Yusuf's final practice report.

Conclusion

Social workers are, of course, not strangers to problem-solving but the educational and management problems stemming from placements can form an unfamiliar terrain. However, guidance on negotiating and navigating this terrain can be made available and, with experience, such difficult terrain can readily be overcome.

Points worthy of note in attempting to tackle these issues are:

1. A variety of support systems are available if the practice teacher is prepared to seek them out.

2. A number of strategies can be developed for preventing problems arising, or for 'nipping them in the bud'. A pro-active approach is therefore strongly recommended.

3. Considerable experience in dealing with placement problems has been built up over decades of practice-based social work education. It is not necessary to re-invent the wheel each time a problem arises. Practice teachers should therefore be prepared to look for the common patterns of problem development whilst balancing these against the unique circumstances of the particular placement.

4. The role of the practice teacher is that of manager of an educational experience. Dealing with difficulties is a key part of management, but this does not imply 'preciousness'. Although the practice teacher has responsibility for the student, he/she is not just 'your' student, as both practice teacher and the student are parts of an overall structure of social work and social work education. Being precious about 'your' student is never a good strategy but, in a problematic placement, it can be disastrous.

Our final comment on problem situations, however, is to reiterate that serious or major problems, although by no means rare, affect only a minority of placements; most are relatively straightforward and provide enjoyable and effective learning experiences for both student and practice teacher.

Chapter 9

Conclusion

For far too long the caricature of social work education has been that theoretical teaching totally unconnected with the 'real world' is done in isolation in the ivory-towered institutions, while the teaching 'on the job', alongside the workers, has been pragmatic, unquestioning and related solely to immediate agency needs. The discussions relating to the possible development of a three-year programme of training went a long way towards identifying what education and training opportunities exist and how these might best be met in 'partnership'. The development of the Diploma in Social Work has built on these foundations.

If we are to form working partnerships, each party must, as Jordan (1984) points out, be prepared to engage in real debate and not aim for an unhealthy consensus. Courses and agencies need to examine what form partnership should take: what each side should gain from it and what each side would have to give up. Academic teachers have to be more accessible to questions about relevance and practical reality, while practitioners need to open up their practice to analysis and critical scrutiny. Education and training are not separate entities to be achieved in the education establishment and workplace respectively. Harris (1984) suggests that there is a place for both in preparing students for work but that, if partnership is to be real, we have to transcend the divide between education and training and see them as a means to an end. Practice teachers are in a position to bridge that divide and have a vital role to play in enabling partnership to work.

A new challenge facing teaching institutions and agencies (and perhaps practice teachers most of all) is the development of new patterns of community care provision and the concepts of purchasing and providing in a welfare "market". At present, all this bears primarily on those dealing with adult clients in social services departments, but already there are indications that the model which is evolving may be extended to work with children and families, and to a lesser extent, with offenders.

At the heart of the new system is the separation of, on the one hand, assessment of need and purchase of service to meet it, and on the other, provision of service by either independent (private or voluntary sector) agencies or in-house "provider units". A social worker acting as "care manager" will need to decide upon and put together a package of care which reflects not only the client's needs, but the constraints of a defined purchasing budget. A social worker in a provider unit will need to work to a contract agreed with the care manager, but will also need to be aware of the cost of the unit's services – and how this relates to the prices quoted by competitors. All this involves the practitioner in learning new skills and presents a range of problems for the practice teacher.

For example, learning will be taking place while systems and ways of working are still evolving: at the time of writing (early 1994) few local authorities have yet worked out exactly what procedures they will employ. For those in a purchaser role, there is likely to be a shift from personal intervention to meet need to the management of others in doing so – mediated through individual care plans and contract specification, through negotiation with internal or external providers and through subsequent monitoring of delivery. For those in internal provider units, there will no longer be a guarantee of referral from colleagues carrying out assessments: if the local private residential home or voluntary day centre offers a better deal on price, quality or flexibility, that is where the contract is likely to go. For purchasers and providers, money and decisions about its effective use will become more important than has been the case. A new vocabulary, and new concepts of the market or quasi-market, will need to be learned and applied.

Then, too, there are associated dilemmas and issues of professional values and ethics which will need exploration. How can a balance be struck between involving clients in establishing their own needs, and explicit rationing of limited funds? (The government's Policy Guidance both encourages "needs-led assessment", and emphasises the need to establish priorities while working "within available resources"). How can purchasers and providers ensure that the contracts which suit them also suit the client? (The client is not a party to the contract and the ethical standards of the others are his or her only real safeguard.)

Will the new systems provide greater flexibility to meet minority needs by introducing more appropriate providers or will it develop its own rigidities to perpetuate and even intensify inequality? (The market model, as presently developed, is essentially familiar and accessible to white, middle-class male providers; there are real fears among ethnic and other minority groups that this market may exclude those who are not familiar with its conventions.)

The practice teacher may well feel daunted when confronted by this task; to teach new skills and explore new dilemmas, while learning those new skills and facing those dilemmas in an agency environment of change and uncertainty. Fortunately, there are good reasons for taking an optimistic view – all of which have emarged as themes in this handbook.

First, sound professional practice is not based upon narrow competence in carrying out today's tasks, but in a rational ability to apply existing knowledge and thinking in seeking solutions to new problems. Assessment skills may need to be modified, but not re-invented. An understanding of priorities and resource allocation, developed in managing one's own time, can provide a basis for building practice in handling purchasing budgets. Practice teachers, like other social workers and social work students, are constantly learning and the community care and associated changes can be put in perspective as another phase of learning.

Second, practice teaching has long since moved from an apprenticeship model in which the supervisor was the only true source of knowledge, to a managed model in which the practice teacher plans guides and co-ordinates a learning experience. So, if the practice teacher in a purchasing unit needs to provide experience for the student of the provider role, this can be achieved by sub-contracting. Skills in budget management or contract negotiations, understanding of strategic purchasing policies, knowledge of the cultures of private-sector or voluntary organisation may all be best developed by others – inside or outside the host agency. The practice teacher's skills lie in managing the process.

Third, the practice teacher does not work in isolation: some of the available support systems have already been discussed. In particular, the importance of the academic institution should be stressed. Much of the drive towards contracting is based upon precedents outwith the social services departments – in the NHS, in compulsory competitive tendering, in experience of welfare provision in other countries. There is a growing literature, partly theoretical, partly based upon experience elsewhere, which will influence practice over the next few years – and will in turn be inflluenced by that practice. It is the job of the academic institutions to know that literature, to make it accessible to students, to work with practitioners to test its validity. At a time of major change, involving the introduction of radical new concepts and procedures, the case for partnership between academic institutions and agencies, to forge the best possible future practice, has rarely been more evident.

We cannot yet be certain how all this will work out. Even in social work with adult clients of the local authority, change has scarcely begun. Within the probation service it is now a requirement that services:

"take the lead in developing local partnership arrangements and . . . make financial provision for resourcing this work". (from "Partnership in Dealing with Offenders in the Community: A Decision Document", Home Office July 1992)

CCETSW has produced its guidance on curriculum development in relation to Assesment, Care Management and Inspection ("Improving Social Work Education & Training V" 1991) and may need to follow this with further notes on Purchasing and Contracting. New competences seem certain to be needed, with consequent modification of Paper 30. But we believe that whatever develops, the basic approaches to practice teaching outlined in this handbook will remain valid and we hope it will continue to provide useful guidance in adapting to new challenges.

* * * * *

To the uninitiated reading this handbook and considering practice teaching for the first time, perhaps from an outsider's perspective, one might wonder: *Why be a practice teacher?* Certainly the task is not an easy one if undertaken in the full knowledge of the commitment a practice teacher has to make in order to do the job well. At the moment, with a few exceptions, most practice teachers undertake the task while carrying their own workload; good practice, involvement in support groups, liaison with courses, additional training – all put extra burdens on the conscientious practice teacher. We do it because, in its very best form, practice teaching is stimulating and exciting. It offers new challenges on a daily basis to our conceptual and creative abilities, to our personal and professional development. Practice teaching puts us in touch with all the issues alive in social work – power, prejudice, judgement, values, change. However, for too long employers have traded on job satisfaction being enough to justify the individual carrying the additional burdens of the practice teacher role.

To date, no national system has been introduced to resource practice teaching and impressions are of piecemeal, well-intentioned measures emerging to satisfy local conditions. There are advantages and disadvantages to a nationally agreed system of resourcing through, for example accreditation. As a practice teacher, you will need to be involved in local discussions that will enable you and your colleagues to work effectively. You may wish to act collectively as practice teachers in your agency or your area. Some of you will prefer to be involved in wider group discussions that will bring about large-scale change. Every practice teacher has something valuable to contribute to the debate and a responsibility to do so for the future of students in social work education, indeed for the very future of social work itself.

Appendix 1: Information for Practice Teacher - Student Particulars

Part 1 To be completed by student at start of course

Name _____ Date of Birth _____ Sex _____

Address: Term _____ Transport _____

_____

_____ Tel No   **Source of Finance** _____

Vacation _____

_____   _____

_____ Tel No   **Personal Tutor** _____

Education (Please give dates and qualifications)

_____

_____

Employment (Please give dates, duration, use chronological order and include all experience, whether or not directly related to social work)

_____

_____

Voluntary Experience (complete as above)

_____

_____

Specific areas of interest or career intentions in social work

_____

_____

Personal Circumstances (which may affect placements, e.g. medical condition, family commitments)

_____

Part 2   To be completed by tutor and student prior to placement request

A   **Date of Placement:** from _____ to _____

       Holidays _____ Recall Days _____

       Total Placement days _____

       Placement   FIRST/SECOND/FINAL   Year of Course   1/2

                              ASSESSED/NON-ASSESSED

       (NB An assessed placement, 50 days or more, requires a pass/fail recommen-
       dation; a non-assessed placement does not, but a practice teacher's report is
       still needed)

Academic Work required during placement

_____

_____

Practice Teacher's role in this

_____

_____

Police Clearance Forms   Enclosed _____ Forms Required_____ Not Needed _____

Description of Placement Sought (e.g. child care team, penal establishment, etc.)

_____

_____

_____

_____

Acceptable Alternatives

_____

_____

_____

_____

B

Progress on Course to date (to include identified strengths/weaknesses/interests and stage of development)

_____

_____

_____

Previous Placement Experience

_____

_____

Specific Learning Needs Identified (in relation to placement being sought

_____

_____

_____

Reasons for Placement Choice

_____

_____

_____

Expectations of the Placement (to include both student and tutor expectations)

_____

_____

_____

Other Factors relevant to this Request (e.g. travelling/residence, named practice teacher, specific areas of work or emphasis)

_____

_____

_____

C

Further Information: to include brief details of course programme and curriculum, requirements in terms of assessment and reports, and (in the case of final placements) copies of earlier placement reports will normally be provided at a contract visit prior to placement, but may be made available earlier if requested.

Contact with placement will usually be maintained by the student's personal tutor; this is however open to variation and in this case practice teachers will be informed at the earliest stage possible. The course's current practice is to make, as a minimum which can be extended if need arises, one 'contract visit' in advance of the placement, and two in the course of it (one in the case of 6 week placements).

Police Clearances are included with this request in view of the time-factor. Where this is not the case, the agency should return the forms for signature as soon as a placement is offered in principle.

Contracts are drawn up at the pre-placement visit; until a contract has been agreed, any offer made as a result of this request is understood to be provisional.

Signed: Tutor _____ Student _____

Date _____

Part 3 to be completed and returned by agency

Name of Agency _____

Name of Student _____ Dates of Placement _____

We are/are not able to meet this placement request.

If unable to meet it, please indicate reasons (e.g. pressure of work, inability to meet this particular student's needs, etc.), to help in future planning.

_____

_____

_____

If able to meet it, please complete the following sections, to help the student by providing some information about what to expect.

Name of Practice Teacher _____

Address _____

Designation _____ **Tel No** _____

Brief Description of Agency or Team (to include, e.g. type of area served, clientele, any special features)

_____

_____

(It will be helpful if any available leaflets, philosophy documents, etc. can be included)

Experience offered to Student

_____

_____

Practice Teacher Experience & Special Interests

_____

_____

Police Clearances   Received _____   Forms enclosed _____   Not needed _____

Please return to: _____ **Signed** _____

Appendix 2: Contract Proforma

Contract for First/Second/Final * Placement
(* Delete as applicable)

Student:

Practice Teacher:

Tutor:

Location of Placement:

Dates (including details of any holiday periods):

Hours to be Worked

Date(s) of Recall to College

1. **Aims and Objectives of Placement**

   (i)   General Expectations of Placement:

   (ii) Specific goals, to include learning needs identified from previous placement, where applicable:

2. **Type of work to be offered/sought:**

3. **Supervision Arrangements:**

   Substitute Supervisor in event of Practice Teacher's absence:

4. **Administrative Arrangements:**

'

5. **Methods of Assessment:**

Interim Report due by:

Assessment Report due by:

6. **Tutor's Input to Placement:**

7. **Additional Points agreed by Student, Practice Teacher and Tutor:**

Summary/Conclusion of Contract:

Signed:

Student: _____ Practice Teacher: _____ Tutor: _____

Date: _____

---

9. Subsequent Agreed Modifications to the above Contract

Signed:

Student: _____ Practice Teacher: _____ Tutor: _____

Date: _____

Appendix 3: Evaluation Report

Final Report

Both practice teacher and student are required to contribute to the final report.

Practice Teacher's Contribution

The practice teacher is required to assess the student's performance in the eight core areas of practice listed below. In assessing performance, guidance is provided in the 'Indicators for Assessment' (pp 83-91). To pass the placement, the student must pass in each of the core areas; failure in any area implies failure of the whole placement.

Core Areas of Practice

> Professional Values and Attitudes
> Communication Skills
> Assessment Skills
> Intervention Skills
> Ability to relate Theory to Practice
> Use of Supervision
> Self-Management Skills
> Ability to Work within Agency Framework

Practice teachers are requested to use these headings in their reports. In addition, they are asked to include in their reports the following information:

a) **Setting** - a brief description of the agency, showing the clientele it serves, any significant features of philosophy and organisation, and the learning opportunities it offers students.

b) **Work allocated** - a brief factual summary of work allocated to student e.g. number and type of cases, groups, projects, court attendance, other agencies visited, etc.

c) **Supervision arrangements** - number, duration and frequency of supervision sessions; joint sessions/seminars; extent of involvement by colleagues (where colleagues have had responsibility for oversight of part of student's work, their comments should be included separately in the report).

d) **Assessment methods** - methods used, e.g. records, direct observation, videos, etc.

e) **Recommendations for future development**

Student's Contribution

This should complement the practice teacher's report, and avoid repetition of material contained in that or other sections. It must include an indication of :

(a) the perceived benefits and shortcomings of the placement;

(b) the student's agreement or disagreement with comments, evaluations and recommendations made by the practice teacher;

(c) the student's own perception of his/her future development needs.

As in the case of the practice teacher's report, reference should be made to appropriate evidence to support statements. In particular, the student must provide examples of the more significant work undertaken, selected (in consultation with practice teacher and tutor) to show its variety, complexity, theoretical base and learning value.

Each case, group, or project selected should be concisely described under three headings:

(a) Account of work carried out, showing initial situation, progress made, and position at closure or transfer, or at end of placement.

(b) Social work methods and skills used in carrying out the work.

(c) Learning involved, to include knowledge/theory/ reading required; skills learned or developed; personal/ professional development involved.

The selection will be influenced by setting. In a conventional fieldwork agency, four pieces of work are likely to be appropriate; in, say, community work a single major project may be all that can be offered, or is required. In all situations, the guidelines are to illustrate, not describe fully, work undertaken, and to show its contribution to learning and professional development. They should be typed if at all possible and concise - normally contained within a total of 3 sheets of A4 typescript.

Appendix 4: Positive & Negative Indicators

1. Professional Values and Attitudes

First Placement

Positive	Negative
Shows awareness of importance of values, beliefs and attitudes on part of both worker and client; recognises significance of power and authority in familial, group and worker/client relationships; flexible and open-minded in matters of value, opinion and judgment; shows commitment to providing an equally valid service to all clients; is moving towards a considered personal and professional value base.	Denies, disregards or fails to recognise contribution of values, beliefs, attitudes; tends to ignore, overlook or be unquestioning of issues of power and authority; is rigid, dogmatic or over-assertive in matters of value, opinion and judgement; allows prejudice or judgemental attitudes to affect work; confuses fact and opinion; advocates, condones or engages in elements of discrimination within practice and policy.

Final Placement

Develops above attributes at a more thought-out level; aware of issues of self-determination and is able to safeguard rights, welfare and choice of others; capable of presenting facts objectively, but does not avoid exercising professional judgement where necessary; recognises and uses tensions inherent in a controlling or monitoring social work relationship; is aware of inequalities in distribution of power in society, can assist clients handicapped by race, gender, age, etc. to combat these.	Still shows above weaknesses, or only limited development of first placement positives. Ignores, denies or underestimates significance of values, attitudes, power, authority; dismisses/ignores client self-determination and other rights, fails to address such issues, or may be overcontrolling; fails to distinguish between use of professional judgement and being judgemental; is inflexible in own values and may try to impose them; believes in ascribed male/female roles and racial stereotypes; believes that issues of race and gender are irrelevant to own practice/professional and self-development; has rigid, dismissive or defensive response to issues of discrimination.

2. Communication Skills

First Placement

Positive	Negative
Listens well, shows good understanding of non-verbal communications (perhaps instinctively). Can express factual information clearly to clients in verbal (and written) form. Can state information and arguments in discussion. Writes straightforward reports clearly, in plain language.	Unaware of clients verbal and non-verbal messages. Finds it difficult to communicate with clients; may be too hesitant, may talk through client, or over client's head. Unable to express ideas in supervision/ discussion. Written reports insufficient in content, confusing in presentation, or inappropriately worded.

Final Placement

Shows all above attributes, but can extend them; conscious understanding and use of non-verbal communications; can interpret complex data and ideas to clients in intelligible form. Can present ordered arguments, based on adequate data and theoretical concepts, in both written and verbal form. Reports are concise yet comprehensive, putting complex issues clearly.	Still shows negative features identified above, or has not moved beyond some of the first placement positive features. Communication with clients or colleagues or other agencies is source of difficulty/ misunderstanding/inadequate delivery of service. Complaints from some or all of these may be feature of work on placement.

3. Assessment Skills

First Placement

Positive	Negative
Grasps the essentials of the client's situation. Can identify main features/contributing factors. Can utilise theoretical material in understanding/explaining situation. Can relate assessment of situation to duties/powers of own/other agencies. Can suggest possible realistic lines of intervention.	Fails to identify significant factors in situation, or makes major errors in assessing their importance. Does not examine situation methodically, or utilise simple theoretical concepts. Assessment/suggestions are unrealistic in terms of client/agency capability, or are not formulated at all; does not move beyond description of situation.

Final Placement

Shows above attributes, but extends them. Can make more sensitive/searching/informed estimates of main features and their significance. Produces assessments which are thorough, accurate as far as can be determined, and provide clear guidelines for intervention.	Still shows features identified above, or has not moved beyond some of the first placement positives. Still omits or gives inappropriate weighting to major factors; may show rigidity of ideas in imposing interpretations. Makes little use of theory in understanding situation. Produces incomplete, inaccurate or unhelpful assessments which do not form sound basis for intervention.

4. Intervention Skills

First Placement

Positive	Negative
Is able to move from assessment to intervention, if not yet at sophisticated level. Can formulate and execute intervention plans, using a base of theory, knowledge of agency function, other resources, and clients' wishes and capacities. Is aware of a range of intervention options, can produce logical reasons for choice made, has some confidence in defending it. Can explain nature and purpose of intervention to client and other agencies.	Is unable to move from assessment to intervention : may prevaricate, endlessly seek more information. Intervention is haphazard/unrelated to assessment/not informed by relevant theory or knowledge. Intervention may be based on too narrow an understanding of methods and options available. Nature and purpose of actions is unclear to client and others/cannot be justified/is wholly tentative and lacking in confidence.

Final Placement

Shows above attributes, but extends them. Draws upon a wide knowledge of theory, resources, agency functions, makes relevant (possibly imaginative) connections between assessment and available options. Consistently follows through, and demonstrates competence in, chosen interventions. In at least short-term work, can justify actions by outcomes (within limits of placement and necessary time-scale of the work); can show improvement in position of clients as a result of interventions.	Still shows above features, or has not moved beyond some of first placement positives. Still limited in understanding of options, and in techniques for carrying them forward. Abandons plans and changes tack without good cause, or fails to modify plans where necessary, misunderstands/over-simplifies/distorts the nature of chosen intervention techniques. Little or no evidence that clients' position improved; may even be worsened by uncertain/inappropriate/incompetent intervention.

5. Use of Supervision

First Placement

Positive	Negative
Attends supervision sessions promptly and reliably; shares in preparation of agendas, and prepares agreed work in advance; participates willingly in discussion, questions when unsure, uses material from reading, colleague debate, etc. as input, and makes use of support and advice given; beginning to initiate discussion, becoming less reactive, can accept and use constructive criticism; recognises structured times for supervision, increasingly confining discussion to these periods.	Gives low priority to supervision; evades by other appointments, late arrival, early finishing; does not undertake/finds excuses for not doing recommended reading, advanced work, etc.; does not make use of advice or note important issues outside of sessions; is passive, unquestioning, accepting, or cannot accept criticism, or is overly anxious, cannot respond to re-assurance; cannot put boundaries on supervision, seeks longer sessions/excessive informal help from practice teacher and others.

Final Placement

Continues to show above attributes, but extends them; shows enthusiasm for expansion of knowledge and ways of working; actively seeks out relevant material from reading, colleagues, other sources of information to promote learning; can transfer learning from one situation to another, and recognise its new application without prompting; actively incorporates wider social work and structural issues (e.g. race, gender) into work-based learning and discussion; sets high value on future supervision as aid to professional development.	Still shows above negative features, or has not progressed beyond some first placement positives; is content with low, basic level of practice, rarely questions, does not take risks in extending self-learning, or see supervision as way of promoting this; unresponsive to teaching, needing frequent repetition/re-inforcement; responds aggressively/resentfully/passively to constructive criticism; cannot transfer learning, or incorporate wider issues into work-based learning; has indifferent or negative attitude to future supervision.

6. Ability to Relate Theory to Practice

First Placement

Positive	Negative
Shows ability (if at a relatively simple and unsophisticated level) to relate practice experience to wider areas of learning; relates agency function to studies of law and policy; uses appropriate sociological/psychological material to further understanding of clients' situation; shows understanding of application of values, theoretical concepts to practice; is beginning to use social work theories and methodology to guide practice.	Tends to divorce theory and practice, or dismiss theoretical knowledge as irrelevant; over-reliance on common sense, past experience, or unquestioned assumptions; lacks awareness of importance of values, theoretical concepts, social work methodology for practice; serious misunderstanding or misapplication of course-based learning.

Final Placement

Develops and extends above abilities; can use theory at more advanced or broader level; shows understanding of a range of theoretical approaches or methods, and similarities/differences between them; has the ability to select, apply and sustain appropriate social work methods to help clients; can demonstrate/make explicit the use of such methods.	Still shows above weaknesses, or has not moved beyond first placement positives. Fails to identify the influence of psychological, social and moral-political factors on situations confronting self, agency and clients; cannot explain/analyse work in terms of theory; cannot use theory with discrimination and consistency to guide work; shows negative attitude towards future learning/knowledge development.

7. Self-Management Skills

Positive	Negative
Understands importance of managing own time effectively, punctuality, ability to meet deadlines, etc.; can make use of diary, etc. as aid to planning and managing work; understands need to plan intervention, develop strategies, establish priorities; can generally manage own time and workload competently, with some guidance.	Evidence of poor time-keeping, missed appointments, double bookings, etc.; fails to make use of diary as method of planning and organising time; tendency to mix up, misplace documents etc.; shows an unplanned, hit and miss approach to social work; needs constant direction, reminders in organising workload.

Final Placement

Extends competence in the above activities; shows clear ability to organise time and work effectively and economically; records succinctly, appropriately and punctually; understands administrative systems and works effectively within them; takes full responsibility for management of own workload.	Still shows above weaknesses, or has not progressed beyond basic level of first placement positives; fails to make effective and efficient use of time and resources; tends to dismiss all administrative matters as "needless bureaucracy", cannot relate own work to agency systems; recording inadequate in content, presentation or timing; lacks patience and forethought.

8. Ability to Work within Agency Framework

First Placement

Positive	Negative
Shows knowledge of, questioning interest in agency function, its relationship to other services and professional bodies; shows understanding of effects of structural disadvantage on agency/worker function; is willing to undertake social work tasks of agency, act as its representative; is accepted by other colleagues as part of agency's working group or team.	Fails to develop sufficiently clear understanding of agency policy, tasks and constraints, and their effect on social work practice; lacks awareness/understanding of impact of wider structural issues; unwilling or unable to represent agency appropriately in formal settings; fails to establish good working relationships with other staff within agency.

Final Placement

Extends above attributes; shows informed and critical awareness of agency function, place of social work within it; has clear understanding of statutory and legal requirements of agency, can fulfil these while safeguarding rights of clients; can question/challenge discriminatory practices appropriately; shows understanding of organisational/institutional theories and their application to the agency; can facilitate, mediate and negotiate on behalf of clients, within agency and with other services and bodies; is effective and positive member of working group/team; is actively aware of group and agency accountability.	Still shows negative features identified above, or has not moved beyond first placement positives; lacks ability to analyse/present critique of agency's social work tasks; fails to incorporate statutory/legal powers and duties into social work task, or is over-accepting and sets aside clients' rights; denies importance of organisational/institutional factors for work of individual or team; unable/unwilling to challenge discriminatory practices; cannot perform representative role in relation to clients; lacks confidence in carrying worker role into formal settings; tends to work in isolation from, or even disrupts, work of team; is unable to recognise need for accountability and consultation.

9. Development as a Social Worker

First Placement

Positive	Negative
Is aware that use of self is one of the most important resources in social work; makes positive use of personal experience as tool for learning, is equally aware of impact of clients' experiences on worker; recognises that own beliefs and attitudes are product of personal experience, is open to discussion of them; shows ability to respond flexibly and openly to those with different standards and value systems (derived from different cultural, racial, religious, sexual or political backgrounds); recognises effect of worker's values/prejudice/bias on professional performance.	Fails to see relevance of own life experience to work, or relies wholly on personal experience; resistant to discussing these issues, or to recognising equal impact of clients' experiences; tends to be judgemental, has a narrow view of behaviour of self and others, may attempt to impose solutions in light of own experience; has difficulty in absorbing new ideas, undertaking personal change/development.

Final Placement

Develops above attributes; seeks to promote use of self through supervision, colleague support, training; contributes to development of others; prepared to examine and re-examine own value base and professional identity; works towards balance of personal/professional ethos, resolution of dilemmas between own beliefs and key issues in social work; can question existing policies and practices, willing to take risks, innovate, evaluate practice. Positive commitment to future professional development and learning, and ability to contribute to development of agency, clients, colleagues.	Still shows above weaknesses, or has not progressed beyond first placement development. Resistant to self-examination, difficulty in dealing with concern about personal feelings; dismissive of ideas of team-building, staff support, and evades involvement in group or team meetings not directly concerned with clients; cannot understand relevance of/need for clarity about key issues/personal values in social work; does not question/participate in formation of agency policies and procedures; cannot/will not consider modifying working methods, or participating in relevant team exercises; low commitment to further training or development.

Bibliography

Boud, D. and Walker, D. (1990) "Making the Most of Experience", Studies in Continuing Education, 12(2)

Brown, A. (1984) "Consultation: An Aid to Successful Social Work", Heinemann, London

Brown, G. and Harris, T. (1978) "The Social Origins of Depression", Tavistock, London

Burgess, H. and Jackson, S. (1990) "Enquiry and Action Learning: A New Approach to Social Work Education", Social Work Education, 9(3)

Butler, B. and Elliott, D. (1985) "Teaching and Learning for Practice", Gower, Aldershot

Caplan, G. (1961) "A Community Approach to Mental Health", Tavistock, London

CCETSW (1987) "Accreditation of Agencies and Practice Teachers in Social Work Education", Paper 26:1, CCETSW, London

CCETSW (1988) "The Qualifying Diploma in Social Work : Statement of Minimum Requirements of Social Workers at the Point of Qualification", Paper 20: 9, CCETSW, London

CCETSW (1987) "Care for Tomorrow", Paper 20: 8, CCETSW, London

CCETSW (1991) "Rules and Requirements for the Diploma in Social Work", Paper 30: 2nd Edn, CCETSW, London

CCETSW (Second draft, undated) "Improving Qualifying Training in Social Work for Intending Probation Officers: A Statement of CCETSW Probation Consultative Group", CCETSW, London

Chomsky, N. (1973) "For Reasons of State", Fontana, London

Cropley, A. J. (1977) "Lifelong Education: A Psychological Analysis", Pergamon, Oxford

Doel, M. and Shardlow, S. (1993) "Social Work Practice: Exercises and Activities for Training and Developing Social Workers", Gower, Aldershot

Dominelli, L. (1988) "Anti-Racist Practice", Macmillan, London

Hall, S., Neary, J., Proctor, P. and Doel, M. (1991) "A Curriculum for Probation Practice", Humberside Probation Service

Harris, R. (1988) "Education and Training: What is the Balance?" Paper presented at the Standing Conference of CQSW courses with Probation Options and Association of Chief Officers of Probation, University of Hull

Home Office Research and Statistics Department (1993) "Information on the Criminal Justice System in England and Wales", Digest 2

Jordan, B. (1988) "What Price Partnership? Cost and Benefits", Paper presented at the Standing Conference of CQSW courses with Probation Options and Association of Chief Officers of Probation, University of Hull

Kolb, D. A. (1984) "Experiential Learning", Prentice Hall, Englewood Cliffs, NJ

Kolb, D. A., Rubin, I. M. and McIntyre, M. M. (1971) "Organisational Psychology: an Experiential Approach", Prentice Hall, New York

Mezirow, J. (1981) "A Critical Theory of Adult Learning and Education", Adult Education, 32(1)

Montgomery, I. and Rea, E. (1992) "Equal Partners?", Journal of Training and Development 2: 4, PEPAR Publications, Birmingham

Morrison, T. (1993) "Staff Supervision in Social Care: An Action Learning Approach", Longman, London

Piaget, J. (1955) "The Child's Construction of Reality", Routledge, London

Rojek, C., Peacock, G. and Collins, S. (1988) "Social Work and Received Ideas", Routledge, London

Sedgwick, P. (1982) "Psychopolitics", Pluto, London

Sheldon, B. (1982) "Behaviour Modification", Tavistock, London

Stevens, R. (1983) "Freud and Psychoanalysis", Open University Press, Milton Keynes

Thompson, N. (1991a) "More than a Supervisor: the Developing Role of the Practice Teacher", Journal of Training and Development 1: 2, PEPAR Publications, Birmingham

Thompson, N. (1991b) "Crisis Intervention Revisited", PEPAR Publications, Birmingham

Thompson, N. (1992) "Existentialism and Social Work", Avebury, Aldershot

Thompson, N. (1993) "Anti-Discriminatory Practice", Macmillan, London

Walrond-Skinner, S. (1976) "Family Therapy", Routledge, London

Ward, L. (1979) "Collusive Coalitions in Triads!", Social Work Today, 43

Index

Abstract conceptualisation, 11-14
Accreditation, 5
Active experimentation, 11-12
Adult learning, 7, 9, 10, 14, 18, 46
Ageism, 16, 20
Anti-discriminatory practice, 6, 7, 15-24, 38, 40, 41, 48, 63-65
Assessment, 11, 14, 38, 43, 50, 51, 56, 58-63, 66, 67, 71, 76, 79, 85-87
Audio recording, 45, 48, 55

Behaviourism, 10, 14
Body language, 52, 55
Boud and Walker, 21
Brown, A., 18, 43
Butler and Elliot, 43

Caplan, G., 37
Care manager, 85, 87
CCETSW, 5, 6, 15-17, 50, 56, 60-64, 66
Chomsky, N., 10
Class, 15, 40
Collusion, 18, 70, 75, 76, 79
Competence-based assessment, 6, 8
Concrete experience, 11-13
Contract, 30-32, 70, 85
Crisis Intervention, 34, 36, 37
Cropley, A. J., 38

Deindividualisation, 18
DipSW, 5, 11, 17, 24, 29, 50, 60, 84
Disability, 15, 40
Disablism, 16
Dominelli, L., 21

Empowerment, 16
Evaluation, 6, 48, 50, 52, 53, 55-57, 59, 61, 82

Family Therapy, 26
Fostering, 32, 41
Freire, P., 21

Gender, 15, 16, 18, 40, 43, 63
Groupwork, 32

Harris, R., 18, 84
Home Office, 20

Infantilisation, 23

Jordan, B. 84

Kolb, D. A., 10-14

Learning cycles, 12
Learning needs, 36, 37, 43, 44, 49, 63, 66
Learning styles, 13, 58
Learning styles inventory, 14
Live supervision, 53-55

Manager(s), 9, 28, 29, 36, 69
Matching, 28
Mezirow, J., 21
Mid-placement review, 69
Minimisation, 20
Moral-political context, 40

NLP training, 18

O'Hagan, K., 27

Partnership, 5-7
Piaget, J., 9-10
Police clearance, 33
Positive and negative
    indicators, 64, 65
Power, 20, 22, 43, 88
Practice curriculum,16, 48
Pre-placement planning, 8, 25
Probation, 6, 26, 27, 29, 87
Problem-solving, 10, 37
Process recording, 51, 52
Professional identity, 41, 73
Provider units, 85
Purchasing unit, 86

Race/ethnicity, 15, 40, 43
Racism, 15-17, 19-21, 63, 82
Reflective observation, 11, 12,
    14
Rojek, C., 19

Sculpting, 48,49, 57
Sectarianism, 15
Sedgwick, P., 19
Sexism, 16, 19, 20, 74, 75
Sheldon, B., 9
Social Services, 6, 11, 26, 29
Social work methods, 4, 47
Stevens, R., 10
Stigmatisation, 23
Supervision, 27, 42-49, 53, 54,
    63, 71, 73, 80, 82

Task-centred approach, 34
Theory and practice, 4, 19, 36,
    64
Thompson, N., 5, 15, 16, 22, 37
Time-management, 39
Tokenism, 18, 64

University of Keele, 6

Values, 62, 88
Video recording, 45, 48, 55

Walrond-Skinner, S., 57
Ward, L,. 70
Workload, 7, 8, 29, 35-41, 69, 80,
    81, 88

Yerkes-Dodson Law, 18, 38